BEYOND
FIVE IN A ROW
VOLUME 2

BY

BECKY JANE LAMBERT

FIVE IN A ROW PUBLISHING · GRANDVIEW, MISSOURI

Beyond Five in a Row, Volume 2
Revised Second Edition

ISBN 1-888659-14-9

Copyright © 1997, 2001 by Becky Jane Lambert
Cover painting Copyright © 2001 by Five in a Row Publishing

Published by:
Five in a Row Publishing
P.O. Box 707
Grandview, MO 64030
(816) 246-9252

Send all requests for information to the above address.

Printed in the United States of America

For Troy
The man of my dreams
and the love of my life

Table of Contents

Finding Your Way Around in
Beyond Five in a Row, Volume 2

We've provided a few simple icons to help you navigate through the teacher's guide quickly and efficiently. There are many lessons about science, history, geography and language arts that comprise the majority of the curriculum that do not have any special or unique identification beyond the section headers. But, there are also a variety of special learning opportunities that invite activities, projects, computer activity, etc. Take a moment to familiarize yourself with the icons below so that you'll be prepared to recognize at a glance the various enrichment activities associated with each unit.

Internet
Connection

Drama
Activities

Career Path

Art

Cooking

Essay
Questions

Getting the Most Out of *Beyond Five in a Row*

Welcome to *Beyond Five in a Row,* Volume 2. You're about to begin a wonderful adventure in education built around the concept that the single most important lesson any child can learn is to "love learning." We strongly believe that if a child successfully learns this lesson, all the rest will follow. *Beyond Five in a Row* is a literature-based unit study built around strong, traditional and delightful children's books. In this volume, you will be exploring two books of fiction and two non-fiction selections. These four books will take one semester to complete.

Unlike *Five in a Row*, you will not be studying specific academic subjects on specific days of the week. Instead, you will be guiding your student into a variety of areas each week. Some weeks will have a heavier emphasis on science while others may have greater emphasis on the fine arts, for instance. What you study each week is a function of what chapters you happen to be studying. Overall, your student will receive a comprehensive education in five principal areas: History and Geography, Language Arts, Science, the Fine Arts and Human Relationships. There are several areas you *will* need to supplement including Arithmetic, and the narrow language arts specialties of grammar, spelling and penmanship. These subjects do not lend themselves to a unit study approach and you'll want to be sure to include them each week.

With this type of curriculum, it is not possible to simply read one chapter every day and do the associated lesson activities. Some chapters are brief and you may very well finish the chapter and all related activities in one day. Other chapters, however, may be either lengthy, or filled with an unusually rich field of learning possibilities. These chapters may take nearly a week to explore thoroughly. Your overall goal is to complete the volume in one semester—approximately 90-100 school days. On average, you'll find yourself covering a chapter every two days or so, but part of the joy of unit study is allowing students to follow their interests. You may find some lesson activities such as a personal journal or a leaf collection, for instance, that continue for weeks as you pursue your studies. Other activities may take only 30 minutes to complete. Remember that our goal as educators is *not* to cram facts into children's brains long enough to successfully complete a test on Friday. Our goal is to help children fall in love with learning, to discover the joy of reading, to learn how to find answers and use research tools, to learn to think critically and to assimilate knowledge in a way that is both relevant and memorable.

Inherent in any unit study is the need for good supplementary resources. You'll be making regular trips to the library as your student moves from topic to topic. While *Beyond Five in a Row* provides a tremendous amount of specific, factual content, it will not be enough to satisfy your student who wants to pursue a subject in greater depth. Find a librarian with a heart to serve rather than one who is simply good at checking out books. Explain your needs and what you are doing and then let her know how much you appreciate her support in helping you locate good resources. Bake her a pan of brownies occasionally or bring her an inexpensive "cash and carry" rose from time to time, along with a nice note or card of appreciation. A good librarian is a tremendous resource to any educator!

You will also want to invest in a good set of encyclopedias. That does not mean spending a great deal of money! We recently bought the entire *World Book Encyclopedia* on CD-Rom for our computer for only $20 after the mail-in $20 rebate offer from a local computer store. And of course, you can locate used encyclopedias at bargain basement prices through classified ads, flea markets and used book stores. For 99% of your student's needs, a 1977 encyclopedia works just as well as a 1997 edition. Expect to pay between $25 and $150 for a set. A good encyclopedia, dictionary and atlas are the links between your curriculum guide and the library. These resources do not by any means *replace* the need for regular trips to the library, but they will substantially reduce the frequency and urgency of those trips. Your student can immediately begin to branch out and enrich their studies using the resources at hand. Later in the day, or later in the week when your schedule permits, you can go to the library to look for specific books on the topic.

You will also want to look for opportunities to continue building a personal resource library as time, finances and space permit. Don't rush out and try to fill your library in one week. Get to know the used bookstores in your area and watch the sale tables at major bookseller chain stores. You can often find wonderful resource books for 25 cents to a few dollars. If it's a quality resource, buy it whether you need it now or not. You will eventually appreciate having a book on trees, another on our solar system, etc.

You will discover as you begin Volume 2, that each chapter of the book you are studying includes a "Parent Summary" for your benefit. If you wish, you can "assign" the chapter reading to your student and use the parent summary so that you'll know what has been covered in the chapter. But we also encourage you to read the chapter aloud *with* your student. You can take turns reading, listen while he reads, or read it aloud for him using your best dramatic voices, vocal energy, etc. There is no right or wrong way to do it. Most likely you'll employ a combination of all these approaches.

One important tool for helping pull a unit study together is a timeline. You can purchase good timelines or you can make your own. A timeline can be as simple as a notebook, binder or scrapbook with each page representing 50 or 100 years. You may want to create an adjustable scale timeline covering 100 years per page up until perhaps 1700. Then you can cover 25 years per page up to 1850 and further expand the detail of your timeline by only covering 10 years per page through the year 2000. Whether you purchase a timeline or create your own, the important concept is to help your student begin to locate the place that each person or event has in history. Everything is either *before* or *after* something else. The Spanish Armada was sunk *after* Columbus discovered the New World, but *before* the Pilgrims landed at Plymouth Rock. Each time your student writes down an entry or looks up a date in his timeline, he will begin making those associations of time relationship. He will also begin to discover what things were happening parallel in history–what music was being written at the same time as which war was being fought all while certain scientific discoveries were being made. The world is all inter-connected and timelines are one of the very best ways of grasping the big picture so important in a good education!

You will find a Writing and Discussion Question for every chapter. We strongly believe that learning to communicate clearly is foundational to any good education. Your student may or may not need to understand the complexities of physics in his chosen career field, but he *will* need to be able to communicate with others through both the spoken and written word. Use these questions as a starting point. Encourage your student to write frequently. If you have another idea for a discussion question, by all means use it instead. Assign the length of each answer based on your student's abilities and age. Younger students or students with learning disabilities may only be able to write 1-3 paragraphs. Older students, or those who excel in writing may want to write 1-3 pages or more. Feel free to adjust the assignment length as you find out what works for you. And don't feel obligated to use the same length every day. You may assign a 100-word essay one day and a 500-word essay the next.

You will find Career Paths to explore from time to time. You may choose to study each of them to a limited degree, to at least learn more about what various professions do. Others that particularly spark your student's interest may merit much deeper investigation including a field trip to meet and interview someone in the profession. Again, use the curriculum in a way that works for you and your student.

To further enrich your student's studies, you will find a reminder at the end of each chapter to check our *Five in a Row* website to see links relating to the lessons. It goes without saying that if you have Internet access you'll want to use wisdom and supervise your student's access to the wide variety of sometimes unwholesome material available in cyberspace. On the other hand, there are wonderful resources available from businesses, agencies and universities that can provide a rich resource for learning. Use wisdom and learn about the Internet yourself rather than just turning your student loose with a modem and web browser!

At the back of this volume, you will find a Scope and Sequence detailing the various academic subjects covered. We suggest you mark off each subject as you complete your unit and keep this list as a part of your student's permanent academic record. You may also want to keep a variety of other documentation including your student's essays, reports and projects. You will also find a certificate of completion for you to sign and date when your student has finished this volume. Again, keep this certificate with your student's permanent academic file.

Thank you for selecting *Beyond Five in a Row,* Volume 2. We hope you have a wonderful time using it. If you have Internet access be sure to visit our website at www.fiveinarow.com to exchange ideas with other *Beyond Five in a Row* users.

Now, welcome to the wonderful world of *Beyond Five in a Row*. You are the leader for this adventure, so gather the children around you and have a great time!

Becky Jane Lambert
December, 1997

SARAH, PLAIN AND TALL
BY PATRICIA MacLACHLAN

Chapter 1

Parent Summary

Our first chapter begins with an introduction to Caleb and his sister Anna. We find out their mother died when Caleb was born, and now the children live with their father, Jacob Witting, and their two dogs, Nick and Lottie, on the great wide prairie. Caleb, longing to know more about his mother and to remember her, asks Anna about the day he was born. Anna tells him the story as best she can remember. Caleb knows that his mother sang beautiful songs, but he doesn't remember her voice or the tunes. Anna says she doesn't either. That night, as the family sits down for the evening meal, Papa tells the children some interesting news. He has placed an advertisement for a new wife— a new mother for Anna and Caleb. The children are surprised, and are further surprised by his following words. He has received a response. He reads the letter from Sarah Elisabeth Wheaton to the children. Sarah sounds kind in the letter and everyone smiles. Anna, with her arm around Caleb, asks Papa in his next letter to find out if Sarah sings.

What we will cover in this chapter:

History and Geography: Maine and the Eastern United States

History and Geography: Prairies—Beginning Your Notebook

Science: Babies and Human Development

Science: Rocks—Three Types

Language Arts: MacLachlan's Use of a Continuing Symbol—Singing

Language Arts: Letter Writing—P.S. and R.S.V.P.

Language Arts: Creative Writing—Writing a Personal Introduction

Language Arts: Avoiding Clichés—Interesting Description

Fine Arts: Composition in Drawing

Issues of Human Relationships: Memories

Issues of Human Relationships: Singing—A Family Activity

Lesson Activities

History and Geography: Maine and the Eastern United States

On page 9 we read in Sarah's letter to Jacob that she lives in Maine. Sarah also notes, "...the sea is as far east as I can go." Draw your student's attention to that phrase. Indeed, Maine is the eastern-most point of the United States. All that is beyond Maine is the Atlantic Ocean. Locate Maine with your student on a United States map. Find Eastport and share with your student that it lies farther to the east than any other city in the United States. At this point, the reader doesn't know what city Sarah is from, but her observation is true. If Sarah is to move to another state, her only options lie further to the west.

Other information regarding Maine can be shared with your student. For example, the capital is Augusta, and Maine's largest city is Portland. The state bird is the Chickadee and the state flower is the White Pine Cone and Tassel. Maine's coast is rocky and sandy, and is dotted by many lighthouses and villages. Because Maine is densely wooded, it is home to a massive wood processing industry. Interesting to note, Maine makes more toothpicks than any other state.

In early New England vernacular, the word 'down' was used to refer to 'north.' To this day, people from Maine are often referred to as 'Down Easters' or 'Down Easterners.' Sarah might have been called a Down Easter from time to time.

If there is interest, continue studying the eastern coast and Maine. Check your local library for information about this region and state.

History and Geography: Prairies—Beginning Your Notebook

In *Sarah, Plain and Tall* and in our study of its sequel, *Skylark*, we will discover and explore many fascinating facts about two specific regions of the United States—the North Eastern seacoast and the prairies. We will learn about the sea, because that is where Sarah is from and we will explore the prairies because that is where the Wittings live. It would be both educational and entertaining for your student to keep a "Prairie" Notebook and a "Sea" Notebook. Your student can include lists of facts gathered from the story, as well as pictures and notes he makes and collects on his own. The lessons will point out facts as well, in the lesson activity sections in each chapter, so you can be sure to catch all of MacLachlan's descriptions.

On page 5, MacLachlan tells us that Papa, Caleb and Anna live on the prairie. In the Fine Arts section of this chapter, there is an art lesson devoted to this line from page 5: "Outside, the prairie reached out and touched the places where the sky came down." It might be appropriate to have your student copy this sentence down as a first entry in his Prairie Notebook and then, if the art lesson is completed from this chapter as well, to include the artwork in the notebook beneath the quote. In this way, he will be starting what will become a continuing project throughout this book and *Skylark*, as well as 'illustrating' his entry with a correlating art lesson.

Encourage your student to decorate the outside of his Prairie Notebook and his Sea Notebook. He can refer to them and add to them as often as he wishes throughout his studies. By the end of your unit studies on these two MacLachlan books, he will be amazed at the number of both beautiful descriptions and scientific facts he has amassed.

As general background information to share with your student, the region known as the 'prairie' in the United States extends from central Texas to North Dakota, including the majority of Oklahoma, Kansas, Nebraska, Iowa, Illinois, South Dakota and North Dakota. In general, a 'prairie' is a flat or slightly hilly region covered in tall, wild grasses. When you live on a prairie, the summers are hot (100°+ F.) and winters are cold (-30° F.). Rainfall is moderate, and although the soil is generally rich and fertile, the lack of rain can make growing crops trying during particularly dry seasons.

If your student has read the classic books by Laura Ingalls Wilder, including *Little House on the Prairie*, he may already be familiar with many of the characteristics of this fascinating region. If your student hasn't read that series, now may be a good time to suggest it as supplementary reading.

Science: Babies and Human Development

Caleb wanted Anna to tell him the story of the day he was born (page 4). He asks what he looked like. Anna says, "You didn't have any clothes on...Not enough [hair] to talk about..." She shows Caleb a ball of pale bread dough and tells him he looked like that.

Babies are fascinating. If your student has an infant sibling currently, or remembers when his siblings were very young, discuss with him how he would describe a baby. Would he compare it to a ball of bread dough, all pale and soft and bald? Have your student write his own idea of an analogy describing a baby. If your student hasn't had the opportunity to be around an infant, perhaps this would be a good time to locate a friend or neighbor with a baby and ask if he could visit.

As a lesson in science, babies can be the appropriate jumping off point for a discussion regarding human development. Learning about the nine-month human gestation period and the changes that occur at each stage would be a wonderful study. Share as much or as little with your student from the following list of general 'baby' facts as is appropriate and then encourage him to make his own 'flowchart' or poster. He can list each stage of human embryo development and then make his own illustrations to correspond.

A Baby in Development

0. Fertilized Egg--The beginning of a baby, conception, begins with something no larger than a grain of sand. Inside that tiny egg is all the 'information' about the baby—hair color, eye color, physical traits (moles, birthmarks, etc.) and much more. (You may wish to explore a simple book on genetics including RNA and DNA from your library as an introduction.)

1. First Two Months—The baby is called an 'embryo.' Cell divisions take place rapidly. By the end of the second month, although the baby is only about one inch long, all his major organs and features are in place. His brain, heart, legs, arms, fingers, toes and a little bit of a nose are formed.

2. Months Three and Four—The baby is now called a 'fetus' and he is floating freely in the special fluid called 'amniotic' fluid, inside the placenta and uterus. He is now about 5 inches long and weighs about two ounces.

[**Teacher's Note**: Help make these measurements relative and relevant by showing your student exact lengths and weights.]

3. Months Five and Six—The baby can move and kick because he is getting stronger. The mother can feel the baby moving and the baby can hear. He can even recognize his own mother's voice. At this stage, babies even suck their thumb.

4. Month Seven—By now the baby is almost 14 inches in length and will begin to turn himself upside down, getting ready for birth.

5. Months Eight and Nine—The baby continues to gain weight and his lungs develop more fully. When he is ready to be born, he will weigh an average of 7 pounds and be approximately 20 inches in length.

When we look at a baby, we notice several things right away. Many babies do not have much hair at all, cry a lot, sleep a lot and grow very fast! When a baby is born, his body proportions are very different from that of an adult. If you look at most newborn babies, you will notice that their heads make up nearly 1/4 of their entire body's length. In contrast, an adult's head makes up approximately only 1/8 of his total body length. As babies grow and develop, this change in head/body proportion is just one of many physical and mental processes that take place.

Take some time with your student and look at pictures of him when he was a baby. How different he looks! Can he find a picture of himself that looks like he does now? Is there a photograph that has an expression or body movement that he still makes or does?

Also, if there is interest, your student may wish to discuss or study in more depth the topic of human sexual reproduction and how the egg and sperm unite. This is a very specific area of study and, of course, is left entirely to the teacher's discretion.

Science: Rocks—Three Types

On page 4, Anna turns the bread dough she has been kneading out onto a marble slab on her table. Does your student know what type of rock marble is? What other kinds of rock are there? Take this opportunity to begin a study on rocks—where and how they are formed and the characteristics they possess.

Almost all rocks in the world (98%) are made up of only eight elements: oxygen, silicon, aluminum, iron, calcium, sodium, potassium, and magnesium. And there are many kinds of rocks! Does your student know there is a kind of rock that floats in water? It is called pumice and it floats when placed in water. The reason a pumice rock floats is that it was once hot volcanic lava, filled with various gases. When the lava cooled, the gas escaped and left rocks with billions of tiny holes that then filled with air. Perhaps you can obtain a piece of pumice rock for your student and let him put it in water and watch it float.

There are three main types of rock: igneous, metamorphic, and sedimentary. Marble falls into the second category, and is a metamorphic rock. Here are some general notes on each type of rock:

Igneous—Igneous rocks are formed when molten/melted rock materials deep within the earth's core (called magma) are forced to the earth's surface (by means of earthquake, volcanoes, etc.) and then cool and harden. Igneous rocks include pumice (the floating rock), basalt, and granite.

Metamorphic—The word 'metamorphic' comes from the Greek word/prefix "meta," meaning to change. Just as the word's origin implies, a metamorphic rock is one whose composition has been altered or changed in some way. For example, slate is a metamorphic rock formed from shale and clay hardening together. Such changes can be caused by heat or pressure. Metamorphic rocks include slate, marble and quartzite.

Sedimentary—Sedimentary rocks are formed from many layers of other substances (various rocks, mineral deposits, plants, animal skeletons, shells) which, as years pass, form rock. Sedimentary rocks include coal, limestone, shale, and flint.

Beginning a rock collection can be a delightful way to learn more about rocks. If there is interest, locate a rock/mineral store in your area and visit. If there isn't a specialized store, a visit to a natural history museum is just as valuable. Be sure to collect samples and learn about rocks found in your area!

Language Arts:
MacLachlan's Use of a Continuing Symbol—Singing

Caleb wishes Anna would sing. He knows, from Anna and Papa telling him, that his mother sang (page 3). He is convinced if they sang the same songs, even now, he could remember her, too. Throughout *Sarah, Plain and Tall*, we will hear the Witting family discuss singing and we will eventually find out if Sarah sings—and what that means to Anna, Caleb and Papa.

Share with your student the idea of a symbol. A symbol is something that represents something else. For example, a graph could be called a symbol. If a child is saving his money for a bicycle and every night he draws a line to the amount he has saved, in relation to the amount he needs, that graph represents his money. It isn't really his dollars and coins, but it shows how much it is growing. The symbol (graph) represents the saved amounts.

Writers often employ a literary device known as symbolism. Coming from the word symbol, symbolism means a phrase, thought, action or set of circumstances which represent to the reader what is happening with the characters and the story. In our story, *Sarah, Plain and Tall*, MacLachlan uses symbolism. As your student will discover, the topic of singing will be a reoccurring theme throughout our story. For Caleb and Anna, singing represents their mother. For us, singing is a "picture" or symbol of how Papa, Anna and Caleb heal from the pain of losing Mrs. Witting and how Sarah helps bring that healing.

For now, just draw your student's attention to the concept of literary symbolism and the times 'singing' is mentioned in this first chapter (first line of the chapter, page 3, page 4, page 5, page 6, page 7, page 10). Then, as the story unfolds over the next several chapters, you can trace the symbolism along with him.

Language Arts: Letter Writing—P.S. and R.S.V.P.

Sarah Wheaton's letter to the Wittings includes an interesting footnote. Sarah writes, beneath her signature, "P.S. Do you have opinions on cats? I have one." Does your student know what 'P.S.' stands for? Where does it come from? Does he understand R.S.V.P. and what that means? To begin, 'P.S.' stands for Postscript—which means 'after (post) writing (script).' P.S. is commonly used by people when their letters are complete, and they find they have something more to add. Like Sarah, who probably remembered after the fact that she wished to inquire about cats.

Another common letter abbreviation is 'R.S.V.P.' Used on invitations, it is actually an abbreviation for a phrase in French. It stands for 'Respondez s'il vous plait' [re spon DAY see voo play] which translates to 'please reply.' If you were to send a party invitation and you wished to know how many people were coming to the party, generally you would include this abbreviation at the bottom of the card, and then people would know to inform you of their intentions.

Show your student an example of each of these abbreviations and encourage him to employ them in his own writing.

Language Arts: Creative Writing—Writing a Personal Introduction

Sarah wrote a wonderful first letter to the Wittings. It was informative and interesting and she *let them get to know her*, even though it was a short letter. It must have been difficult for Sarah to decide what to include in her response to the advertisement Papa put out. She has never met Papa or his children.

Ask your student what he would write to a person he has never met. How would he describe himself? How would he describe where he lives? His family? His interests? What would he put in a P.S.?

As a creative writing assignment, have your student write a letter, similar to Sarah's. He can make up an imaginary person (someone he has never met) and then write a 'Letter of Introduction.' It should be the kind of letter someone would want to respond to—full of interesting information about your student.

Language Arts: Avoiding Clichés—Interesting Description

As always, when you're working with your student on creative writing, you want to encourage him to avoid clichés (for example, 'cold as marble', 'blue as the sky', 'smooth as silk', etc.). Good writers are creative and come up with interesting, different descriptions that capture their readers' imaginations. MacLachlan uses striking imagery and descriptions in this story. Look at page 5, where Anna is remembering the sad day when Mama died. MacLachlan writes, "...remembering the morning that Mama had died, cruel and sunny." Has your student ever thought of the words 'cruel' and 'sunny' together? It is a fascinating description, because it catches the reader off guard, but still accurately describes the scene. Even though the day was bright, Anna saw the light, not as warm or comforting, but as a cruel glare—because of her circumstances.

On page 8 we see another interesting description. "And Maggie had come from Tennessee. Her hair was the color of turnips and she laughed." What is the color of turnips? Perhaps your student doesn't know. When turnips are grown, they have white tops and purple bottoms. We assume our author doesn't mean Maggie's hair was purple! Instead, when you peel turnips and mash them, they are a very pale cream color. What a wonderful, original way to tell us that Maggie's hair is a pale, almost white blonde.

If your student is interested in this description, locate or buy a few turnips and use the following recipe to see what Maggie's hair looked like.

Steamed and Mashed Turnips

1-2 turnips, peeled and diced (2 cups)
2/3 cup water

Simmer for 10-15 minutes, or until fork tender. Drain and mash with some butter and salt. Delicious!

Fine Arts: Composition in Drawing

On page 5, we are given a beautiful description by MacLachlan. "Outside, the prairie reached out and touched the places where the sky came down." What does your student think that the prairie touching the sky would look like?

If your student is younger, simply using this sentence as a title or description for a picture he can draw or paint could be an excellent art lesson in illustration. If your student is older, more skilled artistically, or simply interested in learning new ways to draw more effectively, take this opportunity to share with him a simple lesson in composition, using MacLachlan's wonderful sentence.

By looking at the series of illustrations below it is easy to see a representation of many ways an artist can 'compose' his drawing. Just as a musician can 'compose' a piece of music, so we, as artists, can 'compose' (design and lay out) our pictures. Although visual arts composition can include many aspects, one major area of decision falls in the category known as the 'thirds' rule. Generally, artists compose pictures in thirds. For example, an artist, taking MacLachlan's description, might choose to cover 2/3 of his paper with prairie and 1/3 with sky. Or he could choose the opposite. Most young children, if asked to draw the prairie and the sky, would eye the paper and divide it in half. Seldom does an artist divide a composition directly in half because it makes the work appear less natural. It is more pleasing to the eye and gives a more natural effect to use the thirds rule. However, often artists 'play' with their composition to emphasize various things. For example, if your student read "...where the sky came down" and pictured the sky as massive, he might wish to compose his picture with just a slim strip of prairie at the bottom of the paper and large expanses of sky. Conversely, the picture could be drawn with the prairies reaching nearly the top of the paper and just a sliver of sky at the top.

Share with your student the basic thirds rule and let him try it out, using MacLachlan's line as inspiration. Allow him to adjust the horizons and ratios to create pictures with various impacts.

When this lesson is complete, have your student select his favorite drawing and place it in his Prairie Notebook.

Issues of Human Relationships: Memories

From this first chapter, we can see that Anna and Caleb miss their mother very much. We see Anna's pain that comes from being reminded of things that are now only memories. She can remember the day Caleb was born. She remembers her Mama talking to her. She can remember the singing. Anna has her own set of hurts and longings to overcome, but at least she can remember something.

Caleb, on the other hand, cannot. How sad! To remember something that is gone is painful, but to never know your Mama at all must be worse. That is why he asks Anna to retell the stories, to somehow keep his Mama alive in his heart.

Talk with your student about memories. Perhaps he has had a loved one (grandparent, etc.) pass away and he can remember certain things. What memories stand out? What things have been forgotten? What is your student's earliest memory and how old was he at the time of the event?

Memories that are made with family and friends are wonderful because they allow us to hold on to special times. Make some memories with your student today.

Issues of Human Relationships: Singing—A Family Activity

Obviously, Anna and Caleb's Mama liked to sing. Singing can be a wonderful family time. Singing Christmas carols at Christmas is delightful, but there are other enjoyable songs that can be sung throughout the year. Driving in the car, working in the kitchen, playing in the yard—all sorts of activities can be made more enjoyable and memorable if some songs are shared. Encourage your student to sing more and to learn new songs, as he is able.

Writing and Discussion Questions

In Sarah's letter to Jacob Witting (page 9), she says, "I have never been married, but I have been asked." Why would Sarah include this in her letter? What might she be trying to say?

Vocabulary Words

gestation: the process of having young forming in the uterus

igneous: rock formed by the cooling and solidifying of magma

metamorphic: rock changed in form by pressure, moisture and heat

sedimentary: rock formed from sediment

symbol: something that represents something else

R.S.V.P.: acronym for French "Respondez s'il vous plait." Please respond.

cliché: an overused phrase or example

Internet Connections

To view current suggested links relating to this chapter's lessons, see www.fiveinarow.com/connections.

Chapter 2

Parent Summary

Caleb, Anna and Papa all write Sarah letters. Sarah responds, answering questions about herself, Maine, her cat and her brother William. The children, especially Caleb, enjoy the letters immensely. Papa tells the children that Sarah has offered to come for one month to visit and to see how they all get along. The children eagerly give their consent. The days go by and soon Sarah sends her response. It is short and to the point, "Dear Jacob, I will come by train. I will wear a yellow hat. I am plain and tall. Sarah." Caleb notices an extra line at the bottom of the note. Papa smiles and reads it to the children. "Tell them I sing" was all it said.

What we will cover in this chapter:

History and Geography: North Atlantic Seacoast—Beginning the Sea Notebook

Science: Fog—What It Is and How It Is Formed

Science: Animals—Seals and Whales

Language Arts: Continuing Symbolism—Singing

Language Arts: Reconstructing the Unknown—Learning to Infer

Fine Arts: Illustrating Envelopes

Fine Arts: The Colors of the Sea

Lesson Activities

History and Geography:
North Atlantic Seacoast—Beginning the Sea Notebook

Just as your student should be keeping a Prairie Notebook, he should also keep, as a continuing project for this unit, a notebook about the sea. As our story unfolds, particularly in this chapter, we learn that the sea is an important part of Sarah's life. Throughout the story we gather fascinating facts regarding the colors, animal life, vegetation and culture surrounding the North Atlantic Seacoast—all from Sarah's perspective. Encourage your student to compile as many 'clues' as he can regarding the sea and record them in whatever way he wishes—as lists, illustrations, pictures from magazines he finds, etc.

In chapter 2, we learn several key characteristics of the sea and the environment surrounding it. From Sarah's letters we gather the following facts: The colors of the sea are blue, gray and green (page 11); The sea can be 'fogbound' and a color for which there is no name (page 11); Her brother is a fisherman and catches flounder, sea bass and bluefish (page 11); Whales, seals, and sea birds can be seen (page 12-13); The sea is salty and weathers the surrounding buildings (page 13).

It is obvious that Sarah's home and life are quite different from that of the Wittings who live on the prairie. Anna and Caleb are both aware that Sarah may miss the sea too much, and not wish to stay with them once she visits (page 12). Taking notice of these differences and recording them is an exercise in both observation and cultural enrichment. The author will continue to make occasional notes on the following 'clues' we gather about the sea as our story unfolds.

Science: Fog—What It Is and How It Is Formed

In Sarah's letter to Anna, she describes her brother William, the fisherman and the sea. Draw your student's attention to page 11, and the following sentence: "...he tells me that when he is in the middle of a fogbound sea..." Does your student know what a 'fogbound sea' looks like? Fog can greatly reduce visibility; therefore, William's ship was 'bound,' unable to move safely until the fog lifted. Sailors and fishermen must often deal with weather conditions and adjust their course or plans accordingly. Has your student ever studied fog?

Fog is formed by countless numbers of water droplets that have evaporated from rivers, ponds, lakes or (in William's case) the ocean. As the water evaporates, it expands, cools and becomes water vapor. Air can only contain a specific amount of water at any given temperature. This amount is known as the holding capacity. The warmer air is, the more water vapor it can contain. That is why fog is often seen in the early morning or evening when the air is cooler. As the sun warms the air throughout the day, water vapor is absorbed into the air, and 'fog' is no longer visible.

If there is interest, introduce your student to the four main divisions of fog. They are as follows: Advection fog, Frontal fog, Radiation fog, and Upslope fog.

Advection fog is the type of fog that Sarah's brother William described to her when he talked about the 'fogbound' sea. Advection fog is created when warm air moves over a large body of water and then hits a cooler area (for example, land or a seacoast). The drop in temperature creates fog.

The second type, frontal fog, forms as its name suggests, from a front. When a front (a large air mass of one temperature hitting another air mass with differing air temperature) is formed, raindrops then form, and as they get closer to the ground, they evaporate and form fog.

Radiation fog occurs at night when the ground releases warmth it has absorbed throughout the day (it radiates the heat). When the land cools off, so does the air directly above it. Because cool air can hold less water vapor, fog is formed and hangs close to the ground.

Finally, upslope fog is created as warm air travels in a draft and comes to a hill, mountain or slope. As the air is forced up, it cools. Again, the air's ability to hold the water vapor decreases and fog is formed.

If you live in a hilly area (or mountainous region), your student may have seen upslope fog many times, but not known its proper name. Be watching with your student for fog in your area at different times. Try to determine which of the four types you are seeing.

Science: Animals—Seals and Whales

Sarah names her cat Seal because "she is gray, like seals that swim offshore in Maine." Seals are beautiful animals, and Sarah is fortunate to live where she can see them in their natural habitat. Has your student ever seen a seal, perhaps at the zoo? Or, if you live on a coast, in the ocean? Has he ever touched one? In Sarah's letter to Anna, she also mentions whales.

Encourage your student to spend some time exploring the fascinating world of these two specific sea animals: seals and whales. Use the following information to begin your discussion. If you are able, visit an area zoo, aquarium or the seashore to see these wonderful creatures up close and personal!

Seals are water-dwelling creatures. Most live in salt water (oceans or inland seas), but a few make their home in freshwater. Seals are mammals. They do not have gills (like a fish or shark) so they are unable to breathe underwater. However, seals spend a lot of time in the water and can hold their breath for over 20 minutes! They have hair/fur, are born alive, and nurse their mother's milk when they are born. Seal babies are called pups. (Females are cows, males are bulls, and families are called harems, consisting of many females (3-100) and one bull.) Baby seals weigh approximately 10 pounds at birth, and generally do not leave the harem (or their mother's care) until they are between three and four months old.

The smallest seal in the world is the Ringed Seal. It lives in the Arctic and is generally about four feet in length and weighs around 200 pounds. The largest seal is the Southern Elephant Seal. The males can be as large as 21 feet in length and weigh over 8,000 pounds. The only sea mammal larger than the elephant seal is the whale.

Seals keep warm in frigid waters and temperatures by a layer of fat (known as blubber). Blubber also gives them an energy source when food is scarce.

Seals primarily eat other marine life—fish, squid and octopus. Like birds, seals do not chew their food. Instead, they swallow it whole. As they consume their meal, seals also swallow small bits of shell and rock. These pieces remain in the seal's stomach and aid its digestion by grinding the food up after it has been swallowed.

Seals swim very fast, but they generally are quite slow on land. The Crabeater is the fastest seal and can move (on land or ice) nearly 15 miles per hour—almost as quickly as humans can run.

Whales are also water-dwelling mammals. They are unable to breathe underwater (they do not have gills) but they do nurse their young.

[**Teacher's Note**: Many children think of sharks and whales as the same type of animal, but in reality, they are very different. Whales are mammals. They do not have gills and they nurse their young. Sharks, on the other hand, are large, meat-eating fish. They have gills and can breathe underwater. Sharks and whales also swim differently. A shark's tail is vertical, moving from side to side. A whale's tail lays flat and moves up and down.]

There are 13 different families of whales. Within the families there are more than 75 species. Dolphins, porpoises and whales are all in the whale family. Some of the most common are Orca, Sperm, Beluga and Killer.

A whale is able to hold its breath for nearly 45 minutes when looking for food. Normally, however, whales breathe in air every few minutes. Whales breathe by using a special hole, called a blowhole. A blowhole is a little like one big nostril. When the whale is ready to get air, it comes to the surface of the water and blows out all the water droplets and air in its lungs. This exhale creates a large spray of water and air, known as a 'spout.' The whale inhales a full intake of fresh air. When the whale is underwater, its blowhole is kept tightly shut with muscles, which prevents it from drowning.

A whale's eyes are located on the sides of its head. Although it can see quite clearly both in water and on land, a whale can only see to the side and a little to the back. A whale cannot see anything directly in front of it. Whales have eyelids, just like humans, and can blink, open and shut their eyes just as we do.

When whales are born, their weight and length vary according to species. The Fin whale calf (baby) weighs approximately 3,500 pounds. A Blue Whale calf can weigh up to 4,400 pounds at birth and can be nearly 25 feet in length. The largest whale in the world is the Blue Whale. In fact, the Blue Whale is the largest animal on our planet! Weighing up to 150 tons and longer than 90 feet in length, the Blue Whale is an impressive sight indeed.

[**Teacher's Note**: To help your student gain a better grasp of these various lengths, take some time and help him measure off 10, 20, 40, and 90 feet outdoors. Then imagine a whale that long! Many whales are nearly 20 times as tall as your student.]

Enjoy studying both seals and whales with your student. They are truly beautiful and amazing creatures of the sea!

Language Arts: Continuing Symbolism—Singing

Draw your student's attention to the final sentence in chapter 2 (page 15). Once again, we see the subject of singing taking a role in our story. Sarah may have understood why the children asked that question. Or perhaps she did not. What we do know is that for Caleb and Anna, learning that Sarah sings is a special thing. Before they have even met her, they already feel a bond with Sarah because her ability to sing reminds them of their mother.

Language Arts: Reconstructing the Unknown—Learning to Infer

From Sarah's letters on pages 11 and 13, the reader can infer what Caleb's and Anna's letters must have asked. Invite your student to study Sarah's notes and from them, reconstruct the children's letters. Her letter to Anna includes the following facts:

Sarah can: braid hair, make stew
Sarah likes to: build bookshelves and paint
Favorite colors: blue, gray and green
William, brother: fisherman

Sarah's letter to Caleb includes these notes:

Her cat: Seal, gray like the seals in the sea
She encloses: Seal's paw prints in return
She compliments: the Wittings' house
Sarah's house: tall, shingles made gray from the salt in the sea
Sarah likes: small rooms sometimes
Sarah can: keep a fire going at night
Sarah doesn't know: whether or not she snores

Using these responses, have your student write the letters from the character's point of view (Anna and Caleb) as they might have written them. The following is an example of what Caleb might have written:

Dear Sarah,

My name is Caleb Witting. We have two dogs, Nick and Lottie. Here are their paw prints for Seal to see. Our house is in the prairie, far from anyone and it isn't very large. Do you mind small rooms, Sarah? What is your house like in Maine? It gets cold here in the winter. Do you know how to keep a fire going? One more thing, do you snore?

Yours,
Caleb

As a creative exercise, have your student write his 'letters' on stationery. He can even address envelopes to Caleb and Anna, including a return address from Sarah. If he wishes, he could also draw or stamp the likeness of a paw print from Seal, and two from Lottie and Nick. Have him include the imaginary correspondence in the Prairie Notebook and Sea notebook, respectively. This will not only be a delightful activity, but will also aid in bringing his study of *Sarah, Plain and Tall* to life.

Fine Arts: Illustrating Envelopes

On page 12, we learn that Sarah drew a picture of a cat on the outside of Caleb's envelope. How delightful! Has your student ever sent someone a letter and drawn or painted a picture on the envelope? Take some time and enjoy a wonderful art experience with your student by taking Sarah's suggestion. The possibilities are endless: a self-portrait, a picture of a friend or relative, flowers, vines, a ship at sea with waves lapping at the envelope's edges, etc. Perhaps your student could write a letter to a grandparent, father or mother (tucked in the car for them to find in the morning) or to a friend. He could 'illuminate' the envelope with drawings. Allow your student's creativity to blossom. You could even write a letter yourself and illustrate an envelope for a friend and join in the fun!

Fine Arts: The Colors of the Sea

Sarah tells Anna she loves the colors of the sea—blue, gray and green (page 11). Create a memorable art project by having your student draw a picture (with colored pencils, paints, pastels or crayons), using only these colors. Talk with your student about the many different values, shades and combinations these three colors can create when mixed. In fact, Sarah probably never saw the sea look one specific color, but always a combination of the three. What does the picture look like when it is completed, using the colors of the sea?

On page 11, Sarah also tells us the sea sometimes is a color "which has no name." What does that look like? What does your student think that could be? Play with the colors, and create some "nameless" hues with your student.

Writing and Discussion Questions

When Caleb writes to Sarah, he wishes to know about things such as snoring and building fires. If you wrote a letter to a relative or stranger who might be coming to live with you, what are the things you would wish to know? If you were Caleb's age, would your questions be different?

Vocabulary Words

advection fog: created from warm air moving across water

frontal fog: formed from two air masses of different temperatures colliding

upslope fog: formed from warm air traveling up a slope and colliding

radiation fog: formed from the ground releasing its warmth at night as the land cools off

holding capacity: the specific amount of water vapor the air can contain at any given moment

blubber: the layer of fat on sea animals like seals and whales

blowhole: the hole located on top of a whale's head through which he can breathe in fresh oxygen and exhale moisture

Internet Connections

To view current suggested links relating to this chapter's lessons, see www.fiveinarow.com/connections.

Chapter 3

Parent Summary

Sarah comes to the prairie by train. Papa picks her up at the station and brings her home. Anna and Caleb wait for her to come and Caleb spots her yellow bonnet first. Sarah is just as she said—plain and tall. Seal is with her in his own special black case. Sarah gives both children gifts from the sea. For Caleb, a moon snail. For Anna, a sea stone, smooth and white. The children think Sarah already misses the sea, but she gets settled and they both hope she will like them and stay.

What we will cover in this chapter:

History and Geography: Prairie Notebook Entries

History and Geography: Sea Notebook Entries

Science: Windbreaks—What They Are and Why They Work

Science: Birds—Hawks

Science: Smooth Stones—Rock Tumblers

Language Arts: Tension—Essential for a Plot

Language Arts: Creative Writing—A Dog's Life

Issues of Human Relationships: Wanting to Be Liked

Lesson Activities

History and Geography: Prairie Notebook Entries

This chapter offers many more entries for your student's Prairie Notebook. Encourage your student to add these and, if there is interest, find pictures of the flowers and animals in a good encyclopedia or field guide. He may even wish to draw and illustrate his entries directly in his journal. Here is just a brief listing of the new 'clues' we find in chapter 3, to prevent any from being missed:

Indian paintbrush (red and orange), blue-eyed grass, Russian olive trees, crows, marsh hawks, woodchucks, gophers, windbreaks and dust.

History and Geography: Sea Notebook Entries

Here are a few more notes for your student's Sea Notebook also:

seagulls, moon snail (shell), sea stone

A nice illustration for this entry might be a seascape picture drawing, including all three of these things—the gull, shell and stone.

Science: Windbreaks—What They Are and Why They Work

As we studied in chapter 1, prairie land is very flat, with few trees. Without hills, mountains or even trees, the wind can blow wildly. Nothing stops it. Wind can be a problem for farmers, ruining crops both by blowing seeds away and by bending and breaking the crops as they are growing. From pioneer times through today, people have created

their own ways of slowing the wind. Known as windbreaks, people have planted long rows of trees between the fields and around their homes. These trees provide resistance to the wind, and beauty, as well.

In our story, Anna and Caleb's Mama had planted a row of Russian olive trees to form a windbreak near the barn (page 19). If you live near the plains or prairie, take your student to see a field and find a windbreak to show him. (If you know where there is a Russian olive tree, show your student that too.)

Can your student think of a coat that shares the same name as the protective tree line in the field? (Windbreaker)

Science: Birds—Hawks

On page 18, draw your student's attention to the following sentence, "I saw a marsh hawk wheel down behind the barn." What does 'wheel down' mean? Do all hawks do this? What kind of bird is a hawk? Take this opportunity to share a little about this bird of prey with your student.

A marsh hawk is just one of many birds in the hawk family. Hawks are known as birds of prey.

[**Teacher's Note**: Other birds of prey are vultures, kites, buzzards, eagles, owls, falcons, and harriers.]

Actually, a bird of prey is any bird that lives on other living animals. However, scientists only use this definition with a particular group of birds that have two defining characteristics. First, they must have long, sharp toenails, called talons. Talons help a bird in several ways. First, they help kill the prey by piercing and striking it. Second, talons allow a bird to hold onto its killed or captured prey. Finally, they help to hold the meal down while the hawk eats it. The second thing a bird of prey has is a large, hook-shaped beak. This special shaped beak helps the bird tear the meat/flesh off the dead prey into bite-sized pieces.

When a hawk sees its prey, it often flies faster and faster toward the ground in a downward spiral. This is what Anna saw—'wheeling down.' All birds of prey spend much time 'circling' slowly in the sky. In this way, the bird can survey a large area of ground and spot animals that represent potential meals.

The hawk Anna saw—the marsh hawk—is only one of many hawks in the world. Like other types of birds, the names of hawks suggest where they're found, or often describe the way they look. Here are some more hawk names: Sharp-skinned, Broad-winged, Red-Shouldered, Galapagos, and the Sparrow Hawk.

Hawks fly fast and see with extraordinary precision. This is what helps them to be such fierce hunters. Some people, called falconers, practice an ancient sport called falconry. Although falcons are commonly used, as the name implies, hawks and even eagles are used as well. Falconers train these birds. In time, they can hunt on command. The birds are each fitted with little custom leather hoods to help keep them calm by making it so they cannot see. When it is 'blindfolded,' it remains quiet and the falcon becomes used to its handler-trainer. The falconer wears thick, special leather gloves, so the claws of the bird won't hurt his arms. Falconry takes bravery, care and much patience.

Hawks are beautiful and fascinating creatures. Find some more books on this topic and enjoy.

Science: Smooth Stones—Rock Tumblers

Anna's sea stone was indeed very beautiful (page 20). How did the sea make it so smooth, so perfect? The constant waves roll the stones back and forth. The stones rub against the sand and other rocks, but the motion of the water against the stone will eventually wear down the edges until they are smooth.

Rocks can be polished smooth without the sea, however. Has your student ever heard of a rock tumbler? Sold in many science stores and hobby shops, rock tumblers can be a source of educational delight for many young, budding scientists. A rock tumbler works on the same principle as the water and sand in the sea (friction). A rock tumbler is a machine with a hollow cylinder, electrically driven to turn over and over. Then, aided by water and coarse grit (just like the sand) it rolls the stones and polishes them smooth. Many rocks can become smooth and beautiful using a rock tumbler. If you are able, secure one of these tumblers and let your student experience the wonder of producing his own polished stones. Be sure to look at garage sales, thrift stores and flea markets. While these machines may cost $40 to $100 new, they can often be found for far less used!

Language Arts: Tension—Essential for a Plot

For a story to be interesting, it must contain a key element—plot. A plot is what happens in the story. Characters tell us whom the plot happened to, while the plot itself is the action happening to the characters. Every plot must contain tension. What's going to happen? What are the characters thinking? What will they do? In our story, *Sarah, Plain and Tall*, tension is created from several directions, but all of it is included in one basic question. *Will Sarah stay?*

Throughout the story, Anna, Caleb, even Jacob wonder this to themselves. As the reader, so do we. Will she miss the sea so much she must return to Maine? Will she learn to love the children and Jacob?

Encourage your student to explore the concept of 'tension' in his own stories. Perhaps if you are reading another book together, he can identify the plot and tension in that story. Every good book will include this element. As a project in storywriting, have your student sit down and develop several storyline plots, identifying the tension in each one. These storylines need only be a few sentences long. For example, one storyline could be the story of a boy who finds a stray dog and keeps it in the garage. Story tensions might include: Will the dog recover from its wounds? Will his parents allow him to keep the dog? Will the dog's owners find the dog and claim it? etc. These kinds of story/plot exercises help creative young writers develop an essential skill.

Language Arts: Creative Writing—A Dog's Life

Our story is written in first person, from Anna's perspective. Although we hear the other characters speaking, we only understand what Anna is thinking and feeling. We can read *her* thoughts. But what are the *other* characters thinking? What about Nick and Lottie, the dogs? What do they think of Sarah? What do they think of Seal? Do they like Sarah? Are they excited at the thought of a woman around the house? How will a cat change their lives?

As a delightful creative writing exercise, have your student write chapter 3 over again, this time from the dogs' perspective. Encourage him to give Nick and Lottie as many specific characteristics and feelings as he can. What breed of dogs are they? What do they enjoy doing? What's their favorite treat? etc.

[**Teacher's Note**: Many classic children's books have been written through the eyes of an animal such as *Charlotte's Web*, *The Incredible Journey* and *The Cricket in Times Square*. Together with your student, explore some of these wonderful stories.]

Issues of Human Relationships: Wanting to Be Liked

Caleb and Anna would love to have a new mother. It is obvious. They are both concerned Sarah may not like the prairie, their home, or even them. This tension is a common feeling. Has your student ever met someone new and longed to be his friend? When you make a new friend you hope he will like you. Making new friends can be scary sometimes. What if the other person doesn't like you? Talk with your student about this insecurity and how to overcome it. Sometimes being shy is the way people act when they are nervous or afraid that they won't be liked. The truth is, not everyone will like us. But it doesn't mean we won't have friends or aren't special. Everyone has someone who loves them. Most of us, if we think about it, have many that do.

Perhaps you've dealt with insecurity in friendships. Discuss with your student how it felt when you experienced it. Certainly, everyone has a strong desire to be loved and liked. Sharing these experiences strengthens our relationships. Share with your student today. And truly *listen* to what he has to say about his own life and dealing with new friends.

Writing and Discussion Questions

Think about an experience you may have had when you met someone new and you didn't know how the two of you would get along. Were you nervous? What happened? Write down your feelings and describe the experience.

Vocabulary Words

windbreak: rows of trees or buildings that provide shelter from the wind

bird of prey: a bird with both talons and a hook-shaped beak, who feeds on other animals

talons: sharp, claw-like toenails

falconry: an ancient sport (still practiced today) where birds of prey are tamed and trained to hunt on command

Internet Connections

To view current suggested links relating to this chapter's lessons, see www.fiveinarow.com/connections.

Chapter 4

Parent Summary

Sarah begins to make herself at home with the Wittings. She shows the children how to dry flowers. She tells them about the sea and teaches them a new word, from Maine—"Ayuh..." It means yes. Sarah cuts Caleb's and Papa's hair. She braids Anna's hair and ties it with a beautiful ribbon. And they sing. Sarah sings "Sumer is icumen in..." and soon Caleb, Anna, and even Papa are all joining in. They sing together and they are happy. But the children still wonder if she will leave and go back to Maine.

What we will cover in this chapter:

History and Geography: Sea Notebook Entries

History and Geography: Prairie Notebook Entries

Language Arts: Continuing Symbolism—Singing

Science: Seashells—An Introduction

Issues of Human Relationships: Traits and People

Lesson Activities

History and Geography: Sea Notebook Entries

Here in chapter 4 we see more sea notes in the story. Here are some terms and references your student may wish to include in his notebook. Can he find more?

Kittiwake, scallop, sea clam, oyster, razor clam, conch, seals, seaside goldenrod, wild asters and woolly ragwort, Ayuh!

History and Geography: Prairie Notebook Entries

Here are some additional possibilities from chapter 4, for your student to copy, illustrate and include in his Prairie Notebook:

Clover, prairie violets, wild roses, bride's bonnet, sheep and meadowlark.

Language Arts: Continuing Symbolism—Singing

Has your student been following the symbolism of singing? In chapter 4, we see the characters finally taking part in a song together. This is a symbol of good things. Draw your student's attention to page 7 in chapter 1. Caleb asks Papa, "You don't sing anymore. Why?" And Papa answers, "I've forgotten the old songs. But maybe there's a way to remember them."

Now in chapter 4 (page 26), Sarah, Caleb and Anna all sing, including Papa. And we read, "...even Papa, who sang as if he had never stopped singing."

The fact that Sarah has brought song back to the Wittings shows us that she is bringing back happiness—the kind of family fun they haven't been able to enjoy since Mama died.

Continue looking for singing references in upcoming chapters. If you haven't made singing a regular part of your family traditions or classroom activities, look for ways to incorporate singing today!

Science: Seashells—An Introduction

Caleb is very fortunate. Sarah brings him a beautiful seashell, a moon snail shell from the sea (page 20). She shares with the children her collection: scallops, sea clams, oysters, razor clam and conch shells (page 22). Does your student have any seashells? Many people keep shell collections, even those who do not live near an ocean or a large lake.

If your student is interested, this would be a good opportunity to introduce and explore the world of seashells. Find a few books from your library or bookstore, look at all the pictures and enjoy the fascination with the variety of colors and shapes found in the shells. Below is some beginning information on shells for your discussion.

Seashells come in a variety of colors and shapes. There is a reason for the diversity. It helps the creature that lives in the shell to hide and blend in with his surroundings. Different kinds of shells are found in specific waters of the world. It might interest your student to know that a person who really knows shells can look at a specific type of shell and tell whether it came from the coast of Florida or the coast of Africa!

Seashells are made of calcium carbonate (limestone). They come in two basic forms: one piece coiled into a spiral-like shape (univalves) and those made of two pieces which fit together tightly (bivalves). Caleb's moon snail shell was a univalve.

When a mollusk (mussels, clams, scallops) grows, so does its shell. The spiral-type shells can even be used to judge how old the animal is by counting the rings in the spiral.

Collecting seashells can be a lot of fun. Even the names of shells are interesting: Green Star, Knobby Top, Bleeding Tooth, Banded Tulip, Baby's Ear and Thorny Slipper. Encourage your student to research shells further and even start some collecting, if he wishes!

In the story, Sarah has Caleb hold his shell to his ear and tells him he can "hear the sea." This is an ancient practice and it is fun! If your student has a seashell (the larger the better), 'listen' to the sea with him and then discuss what the sound actually is. When we hear that wave-like, swishing sound, what we are really hearing is the air inside the shell vibrating in the small space. This is called *resonance*.

Issues of Human Relationships: Traits and People

Draw your student's attention to the top of page 23. Anna tells us, "Papa was quiet and shy with Sarah, and so was I. But Caleb talked to Sarah from morning until the light left the sky." Anna was like her father, but Caleb was different.

If we ask our parents or relatives, they will often tell us whom we favor. For example, has your student ever heard, "Oh, you're so much like your father—a chip off the old block." Or, "You're just like your mother. The apple doesn't fall far from the tree." Does your student agree? Does he think he is more like his mother, or his father? The truth is, no child is exactly like one parent. We are each a combination of both of our parents. Often, however, we do take after one more than the other.

If Anna was like her Papa, could we imagine that Caleb was more like his Mama? If so, what must their Mama have been like? She might have been more outgoing than Jacob. More carefree and talkative—more like Caleb perhaps.

Learning about our traits and where we get certain mannerisms (as well as physical traits) is a wonderful way to connect with our family. Since he never knew his mother, do you think Caleb knows he is like her? Remembering our heritage and sharing similarities is all a special part of growing up with family.

Writing and Discussion Question

Caleb makes several comments throughout our story (twice in this chapter—pages 23 and 25) that he is sure Sarah will stay. We know Anna wants Sarah to stay, but we don't see her saying it. Why might she be more hesitant to vocalize her feelings?

Vocabulary Words

univalve: meaning one opening; used to describe a seashell shaped in a spiral

bivalve: meaning two openings; seashells like clams or scallops

Internet Connections

To view current suggested links relating to this chapter's lessons, see www.fiveinarow.com/connections.

Chapter 5

Parent Summary

Sarah names the Wittings' sheep after her three favorite aunts—Harriet, Mattie and Lou. One evening, Sarah is drawing pictures to send home to her brother William. While she draws, Anna and Caleb discuss with her their very first words. Caleb's was windmill. Anna's was flower. Sarah's was dune. Caleb wants to know what a dune is and so Sarah explains. Papa surprises all of them by showing them a "dune" out of hay near the barn. All four of them happily slide down the "dune" and later Sarah writes to William, "Sliding down our dune of hay is almost as fine as sliding down the sand dunes into the sea." The children are happy to hear her say the words, "our dune."

What we will cover in this chapter:

History and Geography: Sea and Prairie Notes

Science: Birds of Prey

Science: Earth Science—Sand and Dunes

Language Arts: Alliteration

Language Arts: Unfolding Information in Your Stories

Fine Arts: Thomas Hart Benton—Paintings That Roll Like the Sea

Issues of Human Relationships: Grieving—A Natural Emotion

Issues of Human Relationships: Making Others Smile

Lesson Activities

History and Geography: Sea and Prairie Notes

Once again we have more entries for your student's Sea and Prairie Notebooks: dunes, wind, mica, rock cliffs, pine and spruce trees, hay, turkey buzzards, windmills.

Science: Birds of Prey

Just as we learned in chapter 4, a turkey buzzard belongs in the family known as 'birds of prey.' With talons and a hooked beak, buzzards are fierce hunters. Unlike hawks and eagles, many buzzards are known as 'scavengers.' Just as the turkey buzzard fed on the dead lamb in our story (page 28), buzzards enjoy feasting on prey which has already been killed or has died on its own. When you see a group of buzzards (or one alone) circling in the sky, often you will find a dead animal below. Another bird of prey that is a scavenger is the vulture. Vultures very rarely kill their prey, but, instead, feed almost exclusively on the dead carcasses of animals they find.

Look with your student for buzzards or vultures in your area and, if there is interest, take some time to locate pictures of these common and often mentioned birds of prey. You may also want to contact local zoos, nature centers or animal shelters to see if there are vultures or buzzards you can see up close.

Sarah describes her special dune in Maine beautifully, doesn't she (page 29)? "It was soft and sparkling with bits of mica, and when we were little we would slide down into the water." Has your student ever seen a dune?

[**Teacher's Note**: If you live in an area where there are sand dunes, this would be a delightful opportunity to take an afternoon field trip. Get away and share Sarah's experience with your student.]

Dunes require three key elements: sand, wind and something such as trees, houses, or grassy patches to cause the sand to stop being blown. Share with your student some information about the first element—sand.

Sand is actually a scientific term for a specific size of rock—a very small size. If it is a bit larger, it is called gravel and if it is a bit smaller, it is called silt. Sand, geologists have defined, is smaller than 1/12th of an inch and larger than 1/400th of an inch. Sand is comprised of several ingredients, but the main ingredient is silica.

[**Teacher's Note**: If your student is older, you may wish to elaborate more fully on the definition of silica. Silica is part oxygen and part silicon, which are the two elements most common to the earth's crust.]

Depending upon where the sand is located, other ingredients will be present, and those most commonly affect the sand's color. For example, in areas where a lot of coral reefs are located (tropical islands), bits of coral will be included in the sand and will make it pinkish-orange. In areas of the world where great amounts of volcanic ash have been left on the beaches (Greece), the sand appears a dark, bluish-black color.

Take some sand and let your student examine it with a magnifying glass or microscope. What does he see? Probably many different colors and bits. The more sand is rolled by the ocean, sea, or lake, the more perfect and rounded the grains become. Geologists call those grains 'mature sand.' Or, in other words, older sand.

Does your student know how glass is made? Interesting to note, glass is formed by sand heated to extremely hot temperatures. Today, sand is mixed with many different ingredients (soda, lime, etc.) to achieve different types of glass, but the main ingredient is still sand.

The next key elements for a sand dune are wind and some object to stop the sand from blowing any further. The wind direction determines the type of dune.

[**Teacher's Note**: For the older student, here are the specific terms for the four main divisions of dunes: Transverse Dunes, Barchan Dunes, Seif Dunes and Star Dunes.]

As a delightful science experiment, why not allow your student to create his own 'mini' sand dune?

[**Teacher's Note**: This exercise should probably take place outdoors to prevent any major messes.]

Take a five-pound bag of either salt or sugar. Have your student pour it into the lid of a cardboard box or a jellyroll pan (anything with some surface area and small sides will work). That will be your student's 'sand.' Next, he'll need something to stop the wind. Twigs, tilted saucers, teacups, a toy soldier or anything else your student wishes can be placed here and there in the sand. Two or three objects are plenty. And now, all your student needs is some wind. By placing or holding a fan or hair dryer near the tray of 'sand' and experimenting with the distance, your student can see his own dunes being created! Encourage your student to try various 'wind' directions to create differently shaped dunes.

Another great way to see a 'dune' effect, even if you live far from any beach, is to observe the snow in your area after a large snowfall. The granules of ice, which comprise snow, will drift and 'dune' according to the wind direction and beautiful dune-like forms will appear.

Have fun studying sand and dunes with your student!

Language Arts: Alliteration

The author of our story, Patricia MacLachlan, is a master with language. Not only is our story interesting and heartwarming, but the author includes many poetic and literary devices to keep the narrative flowing and sounding beautiful.

Draw your student's attention to the first line of chapter 5 (page 28). "The sheep made Sarah smile."

Two of the five words in this sentence begin with the sound 's.' Have your student say the sentence repeatedly. It's almost a tongue twister, isn't it? Sentences where several of the words begin with the same letter create a literary form known as alliteration.

A famous poet and writer, who used alliteration to his great advantage, was a man named Lewis Carroll.

[**Teacher's Note**: Lewis Carroll was the pseudonym (or pen name) of Charles Lutwidge Dodgson, born January 27, 1832, in England. He was a withdrawn man, who had a speech impediment called stammering. However, he greatly enjoyed the company of children, with whom he felt he could relax and speak more clearly. His stories and poems are still popular today, particularly his most famous work, *Alice's Adventures in Wonderland*. Before he became an author, he was a brilliant mathematician and lecturer at Oxford University. He died of bronchitis in his sister's home on January 14, 1898.]

Here is an example of alliteration in the first stanza of his poem entitled "Size and Tears:"

When on the sandy shore I sit,
Beside the salt sea-wave,
And falling into a weeping fit
Because I dare not shave—
A little whisper at my ear
Enquires the reason of my fear.

The words—sandy, sit, salt, sea-wave, whisper, all include the 's' sound and make an interesting and melodic sounding poem.

Encourage your student to try his own hand at alliteration in either a poem or a few sentences. Remind him to look for this literary device when he sees it being used by MacLachlan in this story and in other reading that he does.

Language Arts: Unfolding Information in Your Stories

When an author introduces a character in a story, he rarely tells the reader all there is to know about that character right away. Instead, bits of information are shared throughout the story. Show your student the following example.

On page 25, in the last chapter your student studied, MacLachlan has Sarah introduce us to her three aunts—"There are three aunts who live near us. They wear silk dresses and no shoes. You would love them." Now, in chapter 5 (page 28), we learn their names. "She named them [the sheep] after her three favorite aunts, Harriet and Mattie and Lou."

Our author, MacLachlan, first introduced the aunts, and then later told us their names. Imagine how boring and tiring it would be if every time a new character was brought into a story, the author wrote pages describing them in detail. Instead, giving us bits of information here and there is interesting and keeps us learning and involved in the author's story all the time.

Encourage your student to write a story in three parts. In each part, have him write a bit more information about the main character (or sub-characters, depending upon the length of the story).

Fine Arts: Thomas Hart Benton—Paintings That Roll Like the Sea

On page 29, we find Sarah making drawings to send to Maine of the things she sees on the prairie. We read, "...drawing of the fields, rolling like the sea rolled." We see Sarah compares the fields of grass to the sea. Take this time to introduce your student to a wonderful artist named Thomas Hart Benton. Benton (1889-1975) was born, lived and died in Missouri. The subjects of his paintings ranged from the common (farmers and fields) to the outrageous (abstract compositions). The thread that ties all of Benton's work together is his rolling, sea-like style. His people, buildings, trees and even locomotives all have a rounded, rolled look to them. If you are able, obtain a book featuring some of Benton's work and show your student an artist's interpretation of his world around him. The author of *Beyond Five in a Row* thinks the character Sarah might have liked Thomas Hart Benton's ocean-like shapes. Encourage your student to try several drawings using Benton's style, causing various objects in his work to be curved, rolling—like the sea! (You might also want to find a book called *The Pumpkin Runner* by M. D. Arnold, illustrated by Brad Sneed. Brad Sneed is a current children's book illustrator whose work has been compared to Benton's. Your student could then compare and contrast these two artists.)

Issues of Human Relationships: Grieving—A Natural Emotion

The Wittings find a lamb that has died and Sarah finds the death difficult to handle (page 28). She shouts and cries. Finally, Jacob has to help her back to the house. Talk with your student about Sarah's display of emotion. Grieving is a natural response to death. Some reactions included in the process of grieving are crying, sadness, loneliness and anger. Even depression can follow the death of a loved one, a pet or even strangers (in a war, tragic accident, etc.).

Share with your student a time when you may have grieved. Then ask him if he has ever experienced a deep sadness. Sarah's response to the lamb's death may seem extreme to some, but for those of us who love animals, it's understandable. Learning about different emotions and realizing our feelings are valid is part of growing up. Reassure your student by discussing the grieving process and share about it from your point of view. Such discussions may help your student understand his own deep emotions and may also help your student recognize and be more compassionate of others who are grieving.

Issues of Human Relationships: Making Others Smile

Jacob knows Sarah is missing Maine—particularly when she discusses the dunes (page 29). He gives Sarah great joy by showing her the "dune" behind the barn and allowing her to experience, in some measure, her memories of Maine's sandy beaches. Listening to others and hearing, through their words, their feelings allows us to make note of what they are feeling and needing. Sometimes, if we are lucky, these mental "notes" can translate into actions—concrete things we can give back to the person to make them smile.

Doing kind things for others is a part of the glorious thing that makes us human. Unlike animals, we can sense people's emotions and then actively participate in helping them feel better. Encourage your student to listen actively to the people around him and then to look for ways to make their lives better. It will be a good thing for others, and will build character in your student.

Writing and Discussion Question

Caleb, Anna and Sarah discuss what their first words were. Does your student know what his first word was? Have him try to find out, and then have him include it in an autobiographical sketch. If his parents don't remember, then have him make up a fictitious word (what he thinks his first word *might* have been) and write a sketch about that.

Vocabulary Words

dune: a mound of sand heaped up by the wind

mica: a very thin, almost transparent mineral that flakes easily

silica: the main mineral component of sand

alliteration: the repetition of the same first sound or first letter in a group of words

Internet Connections

To view current suggested links relating to this chapter's lessons, see www.fiveinarow.com/connections.

Chapter 6

Parent Summary

As summer progresses, Sarah learns more about the prairie and the Wittings. She learns how to plow the fields behind the horses, Jack and Old Bess. She asks Anna and Caleb many questions about wintertime on the prairie.

One day, Sarah and the children are hotter than usual. Sarah takes them for a special treat. All three head off for the cow pond and she teaches the children how to swim. It is a glorious afternoon, and the children fall asleep in the warm grass next to Sarah.

What we will cover in this chapter:

Science: Water Sources

Language Arts: The Newbery Medal

Language Arts: Patricia MacLachlan—Writing About What You Know

Language Arts: Hyperbole—Meaning to Exaggerate

Fine Arts: The Killdeer—A Fine Subject for Drawing

Lesson Activities

Science: Water Sources

On page 33 we read, "The cows moved close to the pond, where the water was cool and there were trees." In our studies of the prairie, we know there are not many trees. Why would there be trees by the pond? (Because the pond is a constant water source.)

Remind your student that although there are large groves of trees (forests), generally in places where water is less plentiful, trees grow by the banks of water (river, creek, pond, etc.).

The next time you see trees by the banks of a water source, remind your student of the cow pond in *Sarah, Plain and Tall*. If you'd like, consider planning a field trip to explore the relationship between trees and water sources. You'll find that trees grow most abundantly along streams and rivers, near ponds and lakes. Use the opportunity to explore tree identification and to enjoy a picnic lunch!

Language Arts: The Newbery Medal

Take a moment and talk with your student about the Newbery Medal. The two most prestigious and famous American children's book awards given each year are The Caldecott Medal (for the finest illustrations) and the Newbery Medal (for most distinguished contribution to children's literature).

The Newbery Medal was established in 1922 as a tribute to the first English publisher of books for children—John Newbery (1713-1767). Each year the winner of the Newbery Medal is selected by a board of the Association for Library Services to Children (ALSC).

Remind your student that although each book selected for this high honor is written extremely well, the nomination does not always indicate the story's inherent quality of content. Your student should always exercise his own discernment to judge a book's story and meaning.

Sarah, Plain and Tall is truly an amazing story. It has been hailed by many critics as the great American children's novel of the 1980s. It is no wonder the ALSC selected this fine book as the Newbery Medal recipient of 1985.

Language Arts:
Patricia MacLachlan—Writing About What You Know

Sarah, Plain and Tall is a beautifully written story. Does your student think the details and characters are realistic? How does he think MacLachlan achieves such realism? When writers begin a project, it is often said that they should write about what they know. In this way, the descriptions and people come from the author's experience and not just from imagination. It has even been said, "Every book is an autobiography." No matter what the subject, an author is always going to put some feelings and emotions in the story from his own life and view.

Patricia MacLachlan, the author of our story, was born in 1938 and raised on the prairie—Cheyenne, Wyoming. To this day, MacLachlan carries a small bag of prairie dirt with her to remind her of her roots. Her 1985 Newbery Award winning book, *Sarah, Plain and Tall*, came from a real story she heard as she was growing up. According to an article written for *Children's Books and Their Creators* (Anita Silvey, Editor), MacLachlan said the idea for Sarah came from her youth. There was an older, unmarried woman who lived by the sea where MacLachlan spent her summers. Then one day she traveled to the prairies, where MacLachlan was born. MacLachlan said, of this event, "This woman left her own roots to help a family preserve theirs...the facts of it haunted me."

Does your student see where MacLachlan may have had a rich reserve of experiences to write from? Both of the prairies and of the sea? Of course, not all writers (nor your student) *always* write about things they know personally. However, many of the great writers often give this as their advice to budding authors. Many feel it is more rewarding to write about the things they knew first.

Encourage your student to begin drawing from his own special past and present for story ideas. MacLachlan did and we are all grateful.

Language Arts: Hyperbole—Meaning to Exaggerate

Draw your student's attention to page 35, where Anna discusses what she loves about the winter. "Papa builds a warm fire, and we bake hot biscuits and put on hundreds of sweaters." Ask your student if he thinks the children and Papa really wear hundreds of sweaters in the winter? Of course not. That is an exaggeration. Does your student know that exaggeration in writing prose and poetry has a special name? When an author exaggerates, it is called hyperbole [hi PER bo lee]. Authors use hyperbole to give an effect. For example, if your student reads, "He was as strong as an ox," that would be hyperbole. Of course the man wasn't as strong as an ox, but it paints a picture for the reader of a very tough man.

Encourage your student to think up and write a list of sentences using hyperbole. For example:

I've traveled over every inch of this world.

The wind nearly blew my face off.

Suddenly, there were millions of ants in the bathroom.

Look for good examples of hyperbole when you're with your student (billboards, television, books, etc.) and point them out. Then, watch for examples in your own student's writings and congratulate him on particularly nice phrases.

Fine Arts: The Killdeer—A Fine Subject for Drawing

As Anna finally floats in the cow pond, lungs full of air, feeling free, she sees crows fly over her head—and then she hears a killdeer cry (page 36). Has your student ever seen a killdeer? The killdeer is a small, slender bird that lives on the prairie. Standing only 10" high, the killdeer makes its nest on the ground and this small bird has an ingenious method of protecting its young. When a predator approaches the nest, the parent distracts the predator by acting as though it's wounded—dragging its wing and crying. The predator, knowing an already wounded bird is an easier catch, is distracted and goes after the parent. After the "wounded" killdeer has lured the predator a safe distance away, it flies off.

Besides being an interesting bird to study from a naturalist's point of view, the killdeer is also an excellent subject for drawing practice. With black and white markings, a slender beak and clean body lines, your student will find it a wonderful wildlife subject to draw. Find a good photograph of a killdeer and allow your student to practice sketching this lovely bird.

Writing and Discussion Question

Why do you think many authors write about their own experiences? How does this affect their stories?

Vocabulary Words

Newbery Medal: The prestigious American children's books award given annually

hyperbole: a phrase or word which exaggerates, used in poetry and writing

Internet Connections

To view current suggested links relating to this chapter's lessons, see www.fiveinarow.com/connections.

Chapter 7

Parent Summary

Matthew, Maggie, and their girls Rose and Violet come to visit the Wittings and to help Jacob plow the fields. Maggie, like Sarah, is a mail-order bride and she understands Sarah's longings for Maine. To cheer Sarah up, and to make her feel more at home, Maggie brings her three red banty chickens ("for eating," she says) and some flowers for a new garden. Maggie and Sarah become fast friends and Sarah is comforted by the understanding of another woman. And just as Anna assumed, the chickens are not for eating—by the evening Sarah already has them in the house and is discussing names.

What we will cover in this chapter:

History and Geography: Prairie Notebook Entries

Language Arts: Character Compilation—Maggie

Issues of Human Relationships: Always Something to Miss

Lesson Activities

History and Geography: Prairie Notebook Entries

Here are a few more entries for your student's Prairie Notebook, taken from chapters 6 and 7: killdeer, crow, banty chicken, wild dandelions, summer roses, zinnias, marigolds, wild feverfew, nasturtiums, dahlias, and columbine.

[**Teacher's Note**: Please remember these notebook text 'clues' are only a few of the things your student might choose to include in his notebook. If he desires, quotes, descriptions, outside research, etc., can all be included to make a more richly diversified study tool and keepsake.]

Language Arts: Character Compilation—Maggie

Although we've heard her mentioned, chapter 7 is our first glimpse of Maggie, Matthew's mail-order bride and the Wittings' neighbor. Authors should give us many clues about their characters. Not just by what they say, but by their actions and how others respond to them. What does your student know about Maggie's character after reading this chapter? Have your student create a "character compilation" by making a list of the clues that he discovers about each character as he reads the story.

[**Teacher's Note**: Encourage your student not to stop at the physical traits or circumstances of Maggie and her situation. Rather help your student to infer and explore Maggie's personality, by way of her actions. Example: She must be a woman of generosity to bring Sarah the chickens and plants.]

Maggie: She lives to the south of the Wittings, with her husband Matthew and their two daughters, Rose and Violet. She comes to the prairie from Tennessee in response to a letter from Matthew, just like Jacob's letter to Sarah. She has blonde, almost white hair. She is industrious (she gardens, hitches horses to plows and knows how to drive a wagon). She is a hard worker (she wipes her face, in the hot sun, leaving dirt on it (page 42)). She is generous (she gives Sarah chickens and plants, helps with the meal and shares her heart). She is compassionate (she understands and empathizes with Sarah). She is practical and wise (she tells Sarah, "There is always something to miss, no matter where you are"). She is optimistic (she tells Sarah to try growing nasturtiums even though Sarah's not sure they'll do well).

Is your student surprised by how many clues MacLachlan gives the reader in her story, even about a minor character like Maggie? That is the sign of a good writer. If your student wishes, he can draw or paint a picture of Maggie (or of Matthew, Rose or Violet) and include it with his assignment.

Issues of Human Relationships: Always Something to Miss

Maggie gives Sarah some very wise advice—a truth to remember (page 40): "There are always things to miss. No matter where you are." Has your student ever moved to a different city or neighborhood? What does he think of Maggie's words? Do they hold true? If you have lived in several places, share with your student specific things you miss. Together, come up with a list of things you'd miss if you moved from the place you live now. Examples: restaurants, parks, neighbors, theatres, events, city holiday traditions, a particular room in your house, etc. To help us avoid disappointment and disillusionment in life, we should remember Maggie's words. No matter where you go, you will miss certain things. Remember, the new place you're going will also hold things you will learn to love.

Writing and Discussion Question

Why did Anna assume Sarah wouldn't eat the chickens (page 39)? What do we know about Sarah that might lead us to the same conclusion? What are her feelings about animals?

Internet Connections

To view current suggested links relating to this chapter's lessons, see www.fiveinarow.com/connections.

Chapter 8

Parent Summary

Sarah convinces Jacob to teach her to drive the wagon. She wishes to go to town alone. Anna and Caleb grow frightened. What if she wants to go to town alone in order to leave them?

Sarah also shocks Caleb by wearing a pair of man's overalls. The rains come and as a storm is inevitable, Jacob decides he should fix the house roof. Sarah, still dressed in her overalls, helps Jacob and impresses him with her ability to do carpentry. Just as they are finishing up, a squall blows in and the winds begin. They sleep in the barn all night long, with rain and hail pelting the roof. In the morning, Papa opens the barn door and they are greeted by land covered in hailstones and windblown grass, but they are safe.

[**Teacher's Note**: This is a brief lesson chapter. Please use this time as a transition period to catch up on any lessons you may have missed previously or to schedule a field trip. (You may wish to combine chapter 8 with chapter 9, which also has brief lessons.)]

What we will cover in this chapter:

Science: Squalls

Fine Arts: Recreating Your Own Squall through Sound

Lesson Activities

Science: Squalls

Has your student ever heard of a squall? On page 47, we see Papa warning Sarah and the children to take cover. Take this time to share with your student the meteorological events that comprise the storm known as a squall.

A squall does not necessarily include a dangerous tornado funnel cloud.

[**Teacher's Note**: However, it is wise to note that the front (or squall line) created by two air masses of different air temperatures can produce a funnel cloud. If a twister forms, the storm is then said to include tornadic activity.]

Generally, a squall includes the following weather components: strong, cold winds, a storm front (one warm air mass colliding with a cold air mass), several brief, but fierce, rain showers, and sometimes hail and snow.

Sarah, Papa and the children are lucky they see the storm coming and are able to get food and the animals and get to the barn in time. Squalls often occur very quickly.

If there is interest, find more books on weather (wind, hail, storms, etc.) for your student to explore.

Fine Arts: Recreating Your Own Squall through Sound

Has your student ever listened to an old-time radio program and heard the sound effects? Or has he ever noticed in a movie that has creaks and rattles that they sound remarkably realistic? Creating sound effects is an art form. Children often do this without even knowing it. For example, a child playing with a toy train will often make all the appropriate puffs, whistles and clickety-clack sounds. Sound effects can also be created which are quite sophisticated by using a computer and digitally enhanced sound bites.

What does your student think Sarah, Anna, Papa and Caleb hear outside during the squall (page 49)? The author tells us there was wild wind, thunder, hail (like stones being tossed) and sheets of rain. How would your student reproduce sounds like that? Encourage him to experiment with different things (i.e., ice chips on a cookie sheet, water through a colander, marbles against a board, a clap against a sheet of metal or tinfoil, a hand fan aimed at the recorder in different directions, etc.)

Once your student has come up with a series of his own sound effects, encourage him to enlist several people to help him in the recording of his 'squall.' Have him delegate each sound effect to a different person and then run several practice 'takes' to see if the storm sounds realistic. Perhaps he wants the wind sound to remain constant throughout the recording and then have the hail, rain, etc., come in at different moments. When he has his sound effects scripted out, and each person knows their part, then the fun can begin.

Using a simple tape recorder, have your student record his 'squall' and listen to what he has created. If there are changes to be made, he can re-record his storm as many times as he wishes.

Writing and Discussion Question

Why do you think Sarah wants to go to town alone? Do you think Anna and Caleb's fears are justified?

Vocabulary Words

squall: a severe storm, including hail, high winds and rain

front: two air masses with different temperatures colliding with each other

Internet Connections

To view current suggested links relating to this chapter's lessons, see www.fiveinarow.com/connections.

Chapter 9

Parent Summary

After the storm, Papa keeps his promise to Sarah and teaches her to drive the wagon so she can go to town by herself. Caleb and Anna are frightened. The only reason the children can see for Sarah's trip to town is to leave them. Why else would she want to be by herself? Caleb begins to cry and suggests plans to keep Sarah with them. Maybe they could tie her up. Or make her sick. Anna quiets him, but she is unsure herself.

On the following day, Sarah gets dressed, kisses each of them and leaves for town. The day goes by slowly. Anna and Caleb's only consolation is that Seal is still with them. Evening comes and the children watch for Sarah from the porch. Then, just like the day she first arrived at the Wittings' home, Caleb spies a cloud of dust and her yellow bonnet.

Caleb shares his worries with Sarah—that he thought she would leave them because she missed the sea. Sarah says she would miss Papa and the children more. Then she shows them her purchases from town—colored pencils for their pictures of the sea— blue, gray and green. There are also candles for dinner time, nasturtium seed for her garden and a book of songs to sing.

[**Teacher's Note**: This is a brief lesson chapter. Please use this time as a transition period to catch up on any lessons you may have missed previously or to schedule a field trip. This would also be a good time to review the work in the notebooks.]

What we will cover in this chapter:

Language Arts: Conclusions—How To Tie Up Your Story

Lesson Activities

Language Arts: Conclusions—How To Tie Up Your Story

Draw your student's attention to the final concluding paragraph of our story (page 58). Share with your student how beautifully MacLachlan ties up the ending. She uses bits of information from throughout the entire story. Take each of the following sentence quotations from the concluding paragraph and assign (or help) your student to find in which chapter in the story each item was originally discussed or where it occurred:

Autumn will come, then winter, cold with a wind that blows like the wind off the sea in Maine. (chapter 6, page 35)

There will be nests of curls to look for, and dried flowers all winter long. (chapter 4, pages 23 and 25)

When there are storms, Papa will stretch a rope from the door to the barn so we will not be lost when we feed the sheep and the cows and Jack and Old Bess. (chapter 6, page 34)

And Sarah's chickens, if they are living in the house. (chapter 7, page 43)

There will be Sarah's sea, blue and gray and green, hanging on the wall. (chapter 8, page 49)

And songs, old ones and new. (Many chapters, including chapter 9, page 58)

And Seal with yellow eyes. And there will be Sarah, plain and tall. (chapter 2, page 15 and the title of our book)

Not every author chooses to end his story as MacLachlan does in *Sarah*, with so many bits of information all together. However, it is always a thoughtful literary choice to select some specific subject or saying that is woven through the storyline, to include in the conclusion of a story. It provides closure and allows the reader to immediately reflect back over the entire story.

Encourage your student to try different ways of ending his stories. Perhaps he can mimic MacLachlan's method of story ending in *Sarah, Plain and Tall*, in a story of his own.

Writing and Discussion Question

Why did Papa allow such a young boy as Caleb to take an axe off to chop wood on page 52? Do you find this unusual? What was different about the time our story took place and today?

Vocabulary Word

conclusion: the ending of a story or situation

Internet Connections

To view current suggested links relating to this chapter's lessons, see www.fiveinarow.com/connections.

THE STORY OF GEORGE WASHINGTON CARVER
BY EVA MOORE

Chapter 1

Parent Summary

Moses Carver, and his wife Susan, live in Diamond Grove, Missouri. The year is 1864. One night, robbers come and steal Moses' slave girl, Mary, and her baby son, George. Mr. Carver is outraged and hires a man named Bentley to go and bring back Mary and the baby. Bentley tries to find the young mother and son, but returns with only the child. The baby is sick and frail. The Carvers decide to keep him, along with his older brother, Jim. The baby will someday become known as George Washington Carver.

What we will cover in this chapter:

History and Geography: Genealogy—Knowing Who You Are

History and Geography: Diamond, MO

History and Geography: Civil War—Beginning Information and Interesting Notes

Lesson Activities:

History and Geography: Genealogy—Knowing Who You Are

Draw your student's attention to the photograph of George Washington Carver on page 4. Take a moment to read the caption together. It says no one, not even George himself, knows the year of his birth. What would that be like? Can your student imagine not knowing what day he was born, or even what year?

Knowing about your past and mapping out your ancestry (family tree) is called studying your genealogy. Has your student ever considered where he gets his blue eyes? Why does his name sound French? Why doesn't he look like anyone else in his family?

To begin learning about your past, it's important to discover all you can about yourself. Encourage your student to make up a personal "portfolio" of his own life. Start with the basics: eye color, hair color, height, weight, and physical build, etc. Next, he can begin recording all he knows about his birth: his full name, the date, year, hospital, what the weather was like, etc. Find baby books, birth certificates, diaries, letters and family pictures to provide more information for your student about what his immediate family is like. Your student can begin to ask a lot of questions. His parents, grandparents, aunts and uncles—all his relatives—can provide him with interesting family anecdotes and facts. If your student isn't sure where to begin with his questions, share the following list of question ideas with him. Answers to these questions will help him gain a better understanding of his immediate roots:

Questions for Parents and Grandparents:

1. What is your full name (as it appears on your birth certificate)?
2. When and where were you born?
3. When and where were you married?
4. What are the full names of your parents?
5. When and where were your parents born?
6. When and where did your parents marry?
7. When and where did your parents die? (if applicable)
8. What are the full names of your grandparents?
9. When and where were your grandparents born?
10. When and where did your grandparents marry?
11. When and where did your grandparents die? (if applicable)

When your student has finished gathering his information, or data, encourage him to begin organizing it some way: a journal, a timeline, a three-ring notebook—anything which makes sense to him in which he can easily display the information.

If your student gets interested in his genealogy and wants to know more than he can obtain from personal accounts, here are some places which can provide more information: libraries, public, private and church census records, state and federal agencies, and cemeteries.

George Washington Carver was never sure of his own birthday. Celebrate with your student the joy of knowing as much as possible about his heritage. Help him get started on his own genealogy today!

History and Geography: Diamond, Missouri

Our story tells us George Washington Carver lives in a town called Diamond Grove in Missouri (page 5). The town's name has since been shortened to 'Diamond,' and a monument to George Washington Carver has been erected there.

Find a good United States road atlas, and help your student find Diamond, Missouri. It is located in southwestern Missouri, a few miles southeast of Joplin. Have your student mark this site on the map. Be sure to notice how *many* states border Missouri and their names. Throughout our story, we will continue to hear of the new places that Carver moved to. Your student can create his own 'geographic timeline' of Carver's life—making note of each new town and state.

History and Geography:
Civil War—Beginning Information and Interesting Notes

The Story of George Washington Carver begins during the time of the Civil War (page 6). This was a time of sadness and division in America's history. If your student is interested, take this opportunity to share some beginning information on the Civil War, and some facts your student may not have heard before.

To begin, the Civil War is also known as "The War Between the States" and "The War of Secession" as well as "The War of the Northern Aggression." The Civil War began on April 12, 1861, when southern troops fired on Fort Sumter. The war was a bloody, terrible event, and lasted nearly four years. It officially ended on April 9, 1865.

Historians debate even today what the exact reasons were for the Civil War, but among the answers are two basic causes—the issue of slavery and the economic/agricultural needs of the South. These two causes are in some ways inextricably linked. The country was divided horizontally—north against south. The South (Confederate) wanted to have slaves. The North (Union) believed it was morally wrong. In 1861, the United States had 19 'free' states and 5 'slave' states. President Abraham Lincoln called our country "a house divided."

General Ulysses S. Grant was the commander of the Union, or Northern armies. General Robert E. Lee was the head of the Confederate, or Southern armies. If your student is interested, either of these gentlemen would make an excellent second course of study to accompany this lesson. Get a good biography or video and share portions of it with your student.

You may wish to explore other fascinating, and more intimate looks at the war with your student including books on women and their participation in the event, and the history of African-American soldiers required to fight in the war.

One great resource book entitled *A Separate Battle: Women and the Civil War* (by Ina Chang, Copyright 1991, Lodestar Books, ISBN 0525673652) talks about the women of the day and how they served their communities. Thousands of women served as nurses, both in hospitals and on the battlefield, and even fought (disguised as men). According to Chang, "Dozens of women were discovered posing as male soldiers during the Civil War, and hundreds more may have done so without being discovered. Women enlisted for many reasons. Some couldn't stand to be separated from the men they loved; others felt they could serve their country best on the battlefield."

Another resource title you may wish to obtain is *Between Two Fires* (by Joyce Hansen, Copyright 1993, Franklin Watts, Inc., ISBN 0531111512). This book explores the rarely-told story of the brave African-American soldiers who fought in segregated regiments through the war. Here is an excerpt: "The black soldiers served even though they would not be afforded the rights of prisoners of war if caught by the enemy, did not receive equal pay, and had little opportunity of becoming officers. They faced the fires of war and hatred hoping that people of African descent in America would finally have the right to 'life, liberty and the pursuit of happiness.'"

[**Teacher's Note**: Although these books may be beyond the reading level of your student, they are both excellent resources for information you can share.]

The famous African-American abolitionist, orator and writer, Frederick Douglass said of this event, "Once let the black man get upon his person the brass letters, U.S.; let him get an eagle on his button, and a musket on his shoulder and bullets in his pocket, and there is no power on earth which can deny that he has earned the right to citizenship in the United States."

If your student is interested, help him locate books, maps, biographies, and other materials about the Civil War to assist his exploration. Personalities that might be of interest include: Abraham Lincoln, Robert E. Lee, Ulysses S. Grant, Clara Barton, Sojourner Truth, Harriet Tubman, and Frederick Douglass.

The Civil War was a tragic time in the history of the United States. It is important to study an event of this magnitude so we can better understand the mistakes we've made in the past, and we can resolve to never make them again. Noted historian and author Shelby Foote once said, "The Revolutionary War created the United States, but the Civil War *defined* us." Much that is both right and wrong with America today has its root in our Civil War. It is a subject worth studying in depth. This subject and its related tangents provide a major section of history in this unit study. Begin with several simple Civil War-related topics now and keep a Civil War notebook to add lessons to in the future.

Writing and Discussion Question

According to our story, Moses Carver did not believe in slavery, but he had slaves anyway (page 7). Why do you think he kept slaves if he truly thought it was wrong? Why didn't he free Mary and her children before? How do you think the story of George Washington Carver's life would have been different if this had happened?

Vocabulary Word

genealogy: the study of the descent of a person from his/her ancestors

Internet Connections

To view current suggested links relating to this chapter's lessons, see www.fiveinarow.com/connections.

Chapter 2

Parent Summary

George is a sickly baby, and he grows very slowly. Even when he is about seven, he is still small for his age. His brother, Jim, helps Uncle Moses out in the fields, but George stays in the house and helps Aunt Susan. George loves being alone in the woods and looking at plants. There are so many things to see and touch! George begins to learn about different plants, and starts to care for Aunt Susan's roses. A neighbor, Mrs. Baynham, stops in one day and notices Aunt Susan's beautiful roses. She invites George to come and help her with the roses at her home. Soon everyone starts asking little seven-year-old George what he thinks about their plants, and he becomes known as The Plant Doctor.

What we will cover in this chapter:

Science: Photosynthesis—How Plants Are Fed

Fine Arts: Making Charcoal Bark Rubbings

Issues of Human Relationships: Stuttering—Understanding More About It

Issues of Human Relationships: Developing Expertise

Lesson Activities:

Science: Photosynthesis—How Plants Are Fed

George understands that plants need sun (page 14). Does your student know why? Plants need three things to live: water, air, and light. Take this opportunity to share with your student the fascinating world of photosynthesis.

First, look at the word in two parts: photo (light) and synthesis (to put together). Photosynthesis is the name for a chemical process by which green plants convert light into energy. Photosynthesis is the main function of a plant's leaves.

Photosynthesis is a highly complex and miraculous process, but it can be understood quite easily if it is broken down into specific steps. To first understand photosynthesis, your student must have an understanding of what is in a leaf.

A leaf is made up, in part, of small cell-like bodies called chloroplasts. By themselves, the chloroplasts would be colorless (and so would the leaf), but inside is a green pigment (a colored substance) called chlorophyll. But how does the plant use these little green-filled cells to make energy?

Every plant needs three things: water, air and light. Air is all around the plant. Remind your student that the chemical makeup of water is two parts hydrogen and one part oxygen (H_2O). When light (energy) is absorbed by chloroplasts, it causes the cells to draw water up from the roots of the plant and into the leaves. As water reaches the chloroplasts, the energy from the light splits the molecules of water and divides the hydrogen from the oxygen.

Next, hydrogen molecules combine with carbon dioxide (the plant gets carbon dioxide from the air around it) and forms a simple sugar-food for the plant. This simple sugar is called glucose. Oxygen left over from the water molecules is released by the plant. It provides essential oxygen for the air we (and other animals) breathe every day.

To help your student understand how the water travels up the cells of the plant, take a piece of celery and cut off the base, cleanly. Now place the stalk in a glass filled with colored water (food coloring is perfect.) Ask your student what he thinks will happen. Leave it for a few hours and then remove the celery. With your help, have your student slice through the celery stalk several times, starting from the bottom. Can he see the colored liquid that has been absorbed by the plant's cells? How far up the stalk did the water travel?

If your student is having difficulty understanding the process of photosynthesis, take some time and help him make a poster or large drawing of each step. Find good library books to supplement your teaching on plants and photosynthesis.

Fine Arts: Making Charcoal Bark Rubbings

George enjoys spending time in the woods and studying the plants around him (page 12). He likes to feel the plant leaves and to look at their interesting patterns.

Has your student ever stopped to look at or feel the bark of a tree trunk? What strange textures and shapes! What kinds of trees does your student have around his house? Help him identify as many as he can and write down the name of each. Next, let him observe and feel the bark of each tree. What does it look like? Can he make a quick sketch? What does it feel like? Have him write down his descriptions and put each with the appropriate tree name.

One way to see the beauty of bark is to make a charcoal rubbing. (You can also use crayons or colored pencils, but charcoal pencils work best. Available at any art or discount store, in the school section.) Lay a piece of white drawing paper against the trunk of a tree, and lightly at first, begin rubbing the charcoal across. Can your student see the design and texture beginning to appear? He may need to go back and forth over the same patch several times until the design is clear. Just make sure you don't move the paper around, only the charcoal. He may repeat these steps on trees that have different types of bark.

After he has completed his bark rubbings, he can assemble his own "Bark Observation" Notebook, by compiling the names of his trees, his own descriptions and the relief charcoal rubbings he created. George would have enjoyed a project like this!

Issues of Human Relationships:
Stuttering—Understanding More About It

Draw your student's attention to page 11. Our author tells us George was small for his age, sickly and that he stuttered when he spoke. Does your student have a friend who stutters? Perhaps your student, himself, has this speech difficulty.

Stuttering is a speech/language difficulty, which usually starts before the age of three. No one knows exactly what causes it. Most people who suffer from stuttering find it difficult to speak clearly on the telephone, in public, or in situations where they feel particularly insecure. More males stutter than females, worldwide, and it is more common in Western societies, higher social groups and more affluent economic groups.

The important thing for your student to remember is that although you might think people who stutter sometimes sound ignorant, they are not! Stuttering has nothing to do with intelligence. You should never make fun of or draw attention to someone who stutters. Being sensitive and patient when you are with someone who stutters will help him gain confidence and relax, which will sometimes ease the stammering.

Stuttering can affect anyone. Some very famous people in the world have stuttered. For example, Winston Churchill, one of the most respected statesmen of all time, stuttered terribly as a child. James Earl Jones, the actor, whose voice has now been called a national treasure, stuttered so severely as a child that he was unable at times to speak at all. This difficulty persisted through his adult life, but through speech therapy he has overcome it and has become famous for his acting and voice.

Encourage your student to be kind to any friends who stutter and people he meets with this problem. And remind him that we *all* have things which are different about us—stuttering is just something everyone is able to notice more easily.

Issues of Human Relationships: Developing Expertise

George is becoming known as the "Plant Doctor" (page 14). He has studied plants and the world around him, gathered his own information and knowledge, and now he can help others learn how to care for their plants—just like he helps Mrs. Baynham with her roses.

Even though George is only seven, he has gained expertise in the area of plants. When you are an expert about something, it means you know a lot about it and can help others. As George proves, you don't have to be an adult to develop expertise on a topic. What is your student interested in? How can he learn more about it? Where can he go and serve the community (or a neighbor) to help others with his knowledge?

Encourage your student today by reminding him that even young children can become experts on topics and can help make a difference!

Writing and Discussion Question

George is fascinated by plants and flowers. That is the area of nature that interests him. What aspect of science or nature has caught your interest? Explain why.

Vocabulary Words

chloroplasts: tiny bodies in the cells of green plants which contain chlorophyll

chlorophyll: the green pigment which fills the chloroplasts, located in the cells of green plants

photosynthesis: the process by which plants convert light and water to a food source

glucose: a simple sugar

expertise: knowing a lot about a particular subject

Internet Connections

To view current suggested links relating to this chapter's lessons, see www.fiveinarow.com/connections.

Chapter 3

Parent Summary

George continues to learn more about plants and animals. He learns to sew and knit from Aunt Susan, and he takes up whittling. Aunt Susan gives him a spelling book and George sits by the fire to study. But there is so much to learn! George wants to go to school, but there are no schools in Diamond Grove for black children. He tries to learn as much as he can on his own.

One day, by accident, George finds himself in Mrs. Baynham's house. She shows him her paintings and George is fascinated. He has never seen a painting before! Quickly George goes home and makes up his own 'paint' from pokeberries. Then with his finger, George paints pictures of flowers on a large, flat rock. George decides he loves plants and painting!

What we will cover in this chapter:

History and Geography: Segregation—A Brief Look

Language Arts: Book Recommendation—*The Secret Garden*

Fine Arts: Juice Paints and Vegetable Dyes

Lesson Activities:

History and Geography: Segregation—A Brief Look

George wants to go to school (page 17). He knows he's learning a lot through his own studies, but he doesn't have all the resources that school would provide. We learn that George is unable to attend school in Diamond Grove because there aren't any schools for black children—only schools for white children.

Take this opportunity to share with your student some background information on segregation and its role in America's history.

Segregation means to set one racial group apart from a larger group or society. The term desegregation means stopping these divisions. In the United States, racial segregation (as we recognize it today) began in the early 1800s. By that time, segregation laws requiring blacks and whites to use separate public facilities—bathrooms, restaurants, schools, drinking fountains, parks, etc.—had gone into effect. These public ordinances became known as the Jim Crow laws. A song featuring a black character named Jim Crow became popular in the 1830s and people borrowed the name for the legislations.

It is important to impress upon your student the painful aspect of these laws. For no other reason besides the color of their skin, African-American people were discriminated against and forced to use separate public facilities. Imagine how humiliating and dehumanizing such treatment would make you feel!

By the 1930s, African-Americans were gaining in the arena of politics, forming groups and speaking out. In 1954 an historic ruling came down from the Supreme Court in the case of Brown vs. The Board of Education. In this landmark decision, the Supreme Court ruled against racial segregation in public schools. All children, of all races, should be able to attend school classes together. This was what George needed but was unable to find 80 years earlier—schools that anyone could attend.

If your student is interested in learning more about segregation and the ways by which the United States has changed some of her most offensive laws, you might suggest studying one or more of the following topics and personalities: Rosa Parks, Martin Luther King, Jr. (winner of the 1964 Nobel Peace Prize), and Plessy vs. Ferguson—1896.

As your student begins to study the history of segregation in America, he will see the phrase 'separate but equal' used again and again. This was the belief and sentiment of many white Americans and of the government. It is important to discuss with your student why 'separate but equal' is not possible. Separate facilities (particularly in the realm of education) are not equal. They can only be equal when each child can attend any school, and have the same texts, teachers and opportunities for friendships.

Part of the beauty of the United States is how widely diverse her people are—immigrants from all over the world have made America their home. It is important to learn how to respect diversity, share common grounds and remember that we are all Americans. Segregation was an ugly and painful time in our history. We must work together to prevent it from ever happening again.

Language Arts: Book Recommendation—*The Secret Garden*

On page 17, we find George helping sick and dying plants get better. He finds ailing plants and transports them to an area in the woods he calls his "secret garden." If your student is interested in plants and gardens, in particular, or just enjoys a good story, the book recommendation to accompany this unit is *The Secret Garden*, by Francis Hodgson Burnett (ISBN 03973063261). The story centers around a young girl named Mary Lennox. Having lost her parents to cholera in India, Mary is sent to live with a distant uncle in the Yorkshire moors. Mary is "lonely and willful," but through extraordinary circumstances she finds "friends, health and happiness."

Your student will become instantly absorbed in this classic tale. It is wonderful for reading aloud even with young children. The story not only teaches wonderful lessons relating to the human experience, but also shares valuable information on flowers, gardening and the joy of working with nature.

Fine Arts: Juice Paints and Vegetable Stains

George enjoys painting with the juice of pokeberries (page 20). He doesn't have paints so he invents his own! Your student may wish to try this interesting art form, by steeping some berries (blueberries, strawberries, raspberries, etc.) in boiling water, straining the juice and painting with it. Or, if he wants to try George's method, he can simply crush the berries and paint with his fingers on rocks or bark. (You may want to suggest rubber gloves if you don't want him to have purple fingers for the next few days!)

A great art activity following this theme involves exploring natural dyes. By taking scraps of white muslin or other cotton fabric, your student can try his hand at vegetable and fruit dyes. Onions, beets, the powdered spice turmeric, and even loose, black tea leaves can create fascinating variations of yellow, orange, and brown dyes. If your student wants to try his hand at fruit dyes, encourage him to experiment with blackberries, blood oranges and strawberries.

[**Teacher's Note**: Warn students about handling fabric taken from the hot water!]

To extract the dye from any of these sources, tie the fruit, skins or spices in a piece of cheese cloth and submerge in cold water. Place your fabric in the cold water and then bring it to a gentle simmer. Stir regularly, and have your student watch the fabric and notice the change in color. When it has reached the desired shade, which may take anywhere from 30 minutes to 3 hours, he can lift the fabric out of the pan. Rinse the fabric in clean, warm water until it runs clear. Allow the fabric to air dry.

Writing and Discussion Question

George is very smart. Aunt Susan tells George he doesn't need to go to school—that he already knows more than most school children (page 17). Do you think it is necessary for a child to go to school to receive a good education? Why or why not?

Internet Connections

To view current suggested links relating to this chapter's lessons, see www.fiveinarow.com/connections.

Chapter 4

Parent Summary

George begins to attend church with Mr. and Mrs. Baynham. He particularly loves the singing. George is also excited about being able to attend Sunday School. Instead of learning about things like math and science, George learns about Noah and the ark. He begins to think he needs to move to Neosho. George will miss Aunt Susan and Uncle Moses, but he has to go to a real school! Finally, the day arrives for George to leave home. Aunt Susan gives him a few corn dodgers, and with his small satchel, George sets out alone for Neosho.

What we will cover in this chapter:

Fine Arts: Choirs and Singing

Fine Arts: Cooking—Corn Dodgers

Issues of Human Relationships: Acting in Determination

Lesson Activities

Fine Arts: Choirs and Singing

On page 8, we learn that George enjoys singing along with the church choir. Has your student ever been involved in a singing program? If so, does he enjoy solos or singing with a group? Take this opportunity to share with your student the basic terms and categories for singing and voice.

Every person's voice is slightly different, but all voices can be classified in three categories: high, mid-range and low. These categories are defined by what is called a voice's pitch. Pitch means the voice's position on a musical scale—what range of notes the person can accurately and easily sing. For women, the category names are soprano (high), mezzo-soprano (mid-range), and contralto (low). For men, the terms are tenor (high), baritone (mid-range) and bass (low). The average voice belongs in either the mezzo-soprano or baritone categories.

Does your student know what allows him to speak? What makes each person's voice different? Why do men's voices generally drop lower than women's? The human voice is produced by two thin folds of tissue (vocal cords) that are stretched across the voice box (larynx) in the back of the throat. When air, or breath, moves those folds back and forth they vibrate, producing sound.

The human male's vocal cords tend to be thicker and wider than that of females. For this reason, the male's voice is generally lower.

In our story we read that George has a 'soft, high voice' (page 22). It is interesting to note that George Washington Carver actually sang soprano (the highest pitch in the choir, almost always sung by a woman or young boy) in his church choir. His voice, due to respiratory problems as a child, was always soft and high. You can access recordings of Carver speaking and let your student listen to his unusual voice.

If your student is interested in learning more about singing, perhaps a field trip to a music hall or event would be appropriate. Can he pick out which voices are sopranos? Basses? If he enjoys singing himself, then getting involved in a choral group or singing lessons might be appropriate also.

Fine Arts: Cooking—Corn Dodgers

George loved eating corn dodgers (page 24). Aunt Susan must have made them especially well, because they were his favorite food. Why not take some time and talk with your student about George Carver over a plate of steaming hot corn dodgers? Here is the recipe:

Corn Dodgers

1/2 cup flour
3 tsp. baking powder
1-2 Tbs. sugar
3/4 tsp. salt
1 1/2 cups yellow corn meal
3 Tbs. melted butter
3/4 cup milk
1 beaten egg
4 strips bacon, fried crisp
2 green onions, finely diced

Begin by frying four strips of bacon in a skillet (cast iron preferred). When the bacon is crispy, remove and either leave the drippings in the skillet (if a cast iron skillet is being used) or transfer the drippings to a glass baking dish. Mix together the flour, sugar, baking powder and salt. Add corn meal. Gently fold in butter, milk and egg. Crumble the bacon and gently stir into the batter, along with the diced onion. Pour the corn dodger mixture back into your hot skillet or the baking dish, and bake in the skillet or 8"x8" glass pan at 400° F. for approximately 25 minutes—or until a toothpick comes out clean. Cut into wedges and serve in a little napkin. Delicious!

Issues of Human Relationships: Acting in Determination

George desperately wants to attend school in Neosho (page 23). Imagine being so young and setting off all by yourself on such an adventure. George has to leave behind Jim, Aunt Susan, Uncle Moses and all of his friends and activities in Diamond Grove. But he is determined!

How would your student define the word determination? It usually means the ability to carry out plans or thoughts for a specific purpose—without distraction. A determined person is focused on a goal. Determination isn't the same as rebellion. George does not run away from home without discussion or good-byes. He doesn't tell his family they are wrong. Instead, he purposely continues to discuss his situation and his desires. He is motivated and seeks input. When a person is acting in rebellion, then he is not open to other people's opinions—he is being selfish. Instead, George acts with determination.

Later in his life, George Washington Carver said, "We are the architects of our own fortune and the hewer out of our own destiny." Talk with your student about this quote and what he thinks it means.

Can your student remember a time when he was focused on a goal? When he exhibited determination? Discuss living with purpose and ways by which each can learn to seek out our goals more effectively.

Writing and Discussion Question

Why doesn't George's brother, Jim, wish to accompany him to Neosho? Jim says he doesn't think he needed an education (page 23). What do you think an education can give you? Why is school important?

Vocabulary Words

vocal cords: two pairs of tissue membranes in the throat, near the voice box

larynx: the upper end of the windpipe where the voice box and the vocal cords are located

contralto: the lowest range in a woman's singing voice

mezzo-soprano: the mid-range in a woman's singing voice

soprano: the highest range in a woman's singing voice

tenor: the highest range in a man's singing voice

baritone: the mid-range in a man's singing voice

bass: the lowest range in a man's singing voice

determination: a great firmness in carrying out a purpose

Internet Connections

To view current suggested links relating to this chapter's lessons, see www.fiveinarow.com/connections.

Chapter 5

Parent Summary

George arrives in Neosho in the setting evening. He hurries to find a place to sleep for the night. He is also hungry, having eaten all of his corn dodgers earlier. Finding some wild berries for dinner, George finally falls asleep in an empty horse stall. The next day, a woman named Mariah Watkins discovers George and takes him to live with her and her husband, Andy. George is overjoyed! This nice couple is willing to let him live with them and attend the school designated for black children as well. Each day after school, George helps Aunt Mariah clean the house and cook for Uncle Andy. Each Sunday, the Watkins take George with them to services at the African Methodist Church. Now George can go inside and listen to the sermons, because this is a church for black people. George decides he wants to be like the minister when he grows up.

What we will cover in this chapter:

History and Geography: Last Names

History and Geography: African Methodist Church

History and Geography: A Quick Comparison—Edison and Carver

Issues of Human Relationships: Sociology—Learning More About Adoption

Lesson Activities

History and Geography: Last Names

George had been a slave, owned by Uncle Moses. Moses and Susan's last name was Carver, so George was known as *Carver's George*. When he made it to Neosho, George became known as George Carver. What is your student's last name? Also called a surname, the last name is a family title, often shared by immediate family members. What would it be like to never have a last name?

Many slaves, just like George, took their owner's surname as their own after they became free. Others chose their own last names—often taken from famous American leaders (Lincoln, Washington, Jefferson) or even as combinations of words (Freeman).

As slaves, black people were stripped of all identity. No personal belongings. No equal education. No last name. Talk with your student about what it would be like to not have a surname. How does sharing a name with your family help to bond you with them? How does it help to shape your own identity?

If your student was a slave and was given the opportunity to choose his own last name, what would it be? And why?

History and Geography: African Methodist Church

George attended an African Methodist Church in Neosho with Aunt Mariah and Uncle Andy. This was a place of worship where black people were not only accepted, but were also on staff. Known today as the A.M.E. (African Methodist Episcopal Church), this denomination is one of the largest Methodist denominations in the United States.

Founded in 1787 by Richard Allen and Absalom Jones, the A.M.E. is still thriving and influential today. In 1787, in the city of Philadelphia, large groups of black Americans began protesting the St. George Methodist Episcopal Church. This church discriminated against blacks and was a segregated group. Allen and Jones were the leaders in the separation from St. George's, and they formed their own group. The church name is intended to remind us that this denomination was founded by people of African descent. The A.M.E. has congregations in all 50 states, Canada, 14 African countries, South America and the Caribbean. With over 3 million members, the church continues to grow and accepts members of all races to attend services.

If your student is interested, locate an African Methodist Episcopal Church in or near your area. Visit a service and see what George found so delightful. If you attend a denominational church, you might also make a project of investigating the history and origins of your denomination as well.

History and Geography: A Quick Comparison—Edison and Carver

Draw your student's attention to page 30. Our author tells us, "George was always asking questions the teacher could not answer." What person does your student think of when he hears this description of George? Who else have we studied that was constantly asking questions? Thomas Alva Edison! Another brilliant scientist we studied in *Beyond Five in a Row,* Volume 1.

If your student is interested, go back and review some of the situations in which Edison found himself at school with his instructors. Note for your student that later in his life George Washington Carver became *friends* with Thomas Edison. Edison even offered him a position to work with him on some research events. Great minds must often think along similar lines!

Issues of Human Relationships: Sociology—Learning More About Adoption

Aunt Mariah and Uncle Andy did not have any children of their own—they were glad to have George around. Although they did not legally adopt George, they took care of him and helped him a great deal. Sometimes, however, couples who either don't have any children or want more, adopt a child. Adoption is a legal process by which a person can take as their own a child who is not biologically his or hers.

Does your student have any friends who have been adopted? Siblings? Perhaps your student is adopted himself. Adopted children are just like other children. They are loved, cared for and are legally entitled to all the same treatments—including the right to inherit property.

Adoptions in the U.S. can sometimes be facilitated by an agency, a lawyer or physicians. Without an agency, an adoption is called a private adoption, and this is illegal in several U.S. states. Agency adoptions take three main steps to be complete: 1) the child must be legally separated from his birth parents, 2) the custody must belong fully to the agency, and finally 3) the parental rights are then given to the adoptive parents along with the child. In agency adoptions, the people in charge of choosing the parents (caseworkers) screen each and every applicant carefully. They understand how important it is to place each baby or child with a family where both the child and the family benefit. Every consideration is taken to ensure a successful adoption. Some people wish to adopt children with special needs and these parents are screened even more carefully.

Note for your student that adoption is not a recent legal creation. In fact, one of the earliest written law codes—the Babylonian Code of Hammurabi (1700s B.C.), included a long section describing the laws of adoption. You might want to learn more about Hammurabi's code. Locate a complete timeline of history and show your student how far back in history the Babylonian civilization existed!

If your student is interested in learning more about adoption and what it involves, contact a local agency and request a tour or information packets. These brochures will answer many of your student's questions.

Adoption is a loving and caring way for children to be a part of a family. It allows families the blessing of one or more children that they may never have been able to have.

Writing and Discussion Question

Why do you think the name of George's school was Lincoln School? Discuss where they may have come up with the name and why.

To view current suggested links relating to this chapter's lessons, see www.fiveinarow.com/connections.

Chapter 6

Parent Summary

George leaves Neosho and his good friends the Watkins, and sets off for Fort Scott, Kansas. He has heard there is a different free school there. George hopes the teacher at the new school will be able to answer more of his science questions. Before he leaves, he and Jim get their picture taken together.

When George reaches Fort Scott he meets a wonderful woman named Mrs. Payne. Mrs. Payne invites George to live with her, in return for cooking meals and helping around the house. George accepts. Soon he is attending school and living happily with the Paynes. But one day, George witnesses a white mob beat a black man to death in town. George is horrified and leaves Fort Scott immediately. He never goes back.

What we will cover in this chapter:

History and Geography: Kansas and Missouri

Lesson Activities

History and Geography: Kansas and Missouri

George is certainly moving a lot, isn't he? This chapter takes our budding scientist from Neosho, Missouri to Fort Scott, Kansas. Take some time and share with your student a few interesting facts about each of these states. If your student is still working on United States geography, take a moment and locate both states on a map.

Missouri [muh ZOOR ee] entered the Union on August 10, 1821. Jefferson City is Missouri's capital and Kansas City is the largest city in the state. Boasting primarily industry and farming, Missouri continues to expand and grow. The name, Missouri, probably comes from a Native American word meaning 'town of the large canoes.' Most states have nicknames, and Missouri is no exception. The most common nickname is 'The Show-Me State.' In 1899, Congressman Willard Vandiver of Missouri was speaking at a convention. He said, "...eloquence neither convinces nor satisfies me. I am from Missouri. You have got to show me." The phrase caught on, and is now used to describe the genuine and somewhat stubborn citizens of Missouri.

Missouri has been the birthplace and home to many famous Americans, including Harry S. Truman, Mark Twain, Walt Disney, Joseph Pulitzer, General John Pershing and, of course, George Washington Carver.

George left both Diamond Grove and Neosho in order to attend school in Fort Scott, Kansas. Kansas is often referred to as the 'Wheat State' and the 'Breadbasket of America' because of its tremendous wheat production. It lies immediately west of Missouri. The Native American Indians who originally inhabited this region were called the Kansa or Kaw, and it is from these names that we get the word Kansas.

Most of Kansas is covered by flat plains. Over 200 different kinds of grasses grow in Kansas and the most prominent flower is the sunflower. Wichita is the largest city in Kansas, but Topeka is the state's capital. President Dwight D. Eisenhower grew up in Abilene, Kansas. You can still visit his birthplace and spend an afternoon in Abilene yourself.

If your student is interested in discovering more facts about Missouri or Kansas, he can obtain books at the library to help him in his search. Making maps, tracing the path of different rivers, showing where the major cities are located—all these activities can further your student's understanding of these two fascinating states.

Writing and Discussion Question

Our book tells us that while George was in Fort Scott, there was "...no one to take care of him. He had to look after himself, earn money to buy his meals and to rent a room to sleep in." How would you feel to be on your own? What could you do to earn money? What do you think you would enjoy most about being independent right now?

Internet Connections

To view current suggested links relating to this chapter's lessons, see www.fiveinarow.com/connections.

Chapter 7

Parent Summary

George moves around from town to town in Kansas, and finally settles in Olathe. He finds a nice couple, Lucy and Chris Seymour, and they take the young boy in. George helps Aunt Lucy with her laundry business each day, and he attends school. When George finishes the sixth grade, he and the Seymours move to Minneapolis, Kansas.

Instead of attending school, George begins to seek out college information. He is sure he can do university level work, if only he can find a college that would accept him. George waits each day for responses from his applications, but there is someone else in town named George Carver. George is always getting that man's mail. He wants to be sure he is getting his own. To clear up the mistakes in mail service, George takes a middle initial for himself—'W.' When his friends joke about the letter, George decides it should stand for something. He decides on Washington. Now George Washington Carver has his own full name.

What we will cover in this chapter:

History and Geography: Postal Service—Learning More

Fine Arts: The Accordion

Issues of Human Relationships: Education—Exploring College Applications

Lesson Activities

History and Geography: Postal Service—Learning More

George wants to make sure he's getting all of his mail. To ensure the proper delivery, he changes his name so it is unique to him. What do we do in large cities where hundreds of people might have the same name? Discuss with your student how he should address an envelope for the mail. What do we include?

Each letter the United States Post Office delivers requires at least five pieces of information to be present on each envelope or package it delivers. The recipient's name, street address (apartment number), city, state (or province), and a ZIP code. Post Office employees say the most critical piece of information is the ZIP code.

Does your student know what his ZIP code is? What does it stand for? What do the numbers actually represent?

ZIP stands for Zoning Improvement Plan. Introduced in 1963, the Zoning Improvement Plan was begun in order to speed the sorting and delivering of the mail. That same year, the Post Office Department introduced a series of two-letter state abbreviations. For example, Missouri became MO. New York became NY. California became CA. These state abbreviations are always written *without* a period following. In this way, the city, state and ZIP code can all fit on the same line.

But what do these numbers in the ZIP Code mean? The Post Office Department has divided the United States into 10 geographic areas. For example, let's examine the ZIP Code 22207. The first number, 2, represents Area 2. Area 2 combines the District of Columbia, Maryland, North Carolina, South Carolina, Virginia and West Virginia. Have your student locate this region on a map.

The next two digits, in this case "22", represent the city area or section. In our case, "22" represents the Arlington area in Virginia. Finally, the last two digits, 07, represent the specific village district, neighborhood, or township where the mail is headed.

In 1983, the Post Office Department introduced four-digit codes, in addition to the basic five-digit ZIP Codes. For example, the *Beyond Five in a Row* author's ZIP Code + four is 64030-4509. The last four digits represent the exact house or apartment for delivery. In this way, there is no possibility for mail delivery error, except for human mistakes. This nine number code is so specific, it is all that is actually required for mail delivery. No name, street or state is needed on the envelope. Does your student know his ZIP Code? His four-digit addition? Find out this information from your local post office. Ask them if mail will reach a specific location with only the nine-digit ZIP Code. If so, have your student write himself a letter. Then seal the envelope, place a stamp in the upper right hand corner, and simply write his ZIP code+four on the front. Does the mail come back to him? What does he think will happen?

George would have probably liked to have had this type of accuracy in his mail service. To learn more about the Post Office System and ZIP Codes, contact your neighborhood post office and ask for more information.

Fine Arts: The Accordion

On page 40, we read that George plays the accordion in school concerts. Does your student know what an accordion is? Has he ever seen someone play an accordion? Explore this new instrument together.

Accordions are perhaps most synonymous with German polka bands. If you are able, try to locate some polka music for your student to listen to. (For accordion music, try Internet sites, the old Lawrence Welk videos, and CDs at larger libraries.) When your student listens, can he pick out the accordion?

Accordions are very unique instruments. Somewhat like a mini-piano, they have a keyboard, which the player plays with his right hand. The player's left hand is used to pump the bellows. As the air is pushed by the closing of the bellows, it vibrates against metal reeds and produces sound. Playing an accordion can be complicated, but the result when mastered, is beautiful.

Watch for examples of accordion music or instruments to point out to your student. As in everything else, George is a special person. Even his musical instrument is uncommon!

Issues of Human Relationships:
Education—Exploring College Applications

George is interested in going to college (page 41). He fills out applications to see if he is accepted. Has your student ever had the opportunity to look over a college application or requirement sheet? Even though it is early for your student to be seriously looking at colleges, it might be fun and informative for him to see exactly what a junior college or university application includes.

What kinds of classes will he have needed to complete? What is a G.P.A. (grade point average)? How is it calculated? What does it mean when a class is described as 'a three-hour class?' What is an 'elective' versus a 'requirement?'

If your student is interested, contact a local junior college or university and request a catalog and application. Then sit down with your student and explore it together. In this way, your student will have a better understanding of the serious choices George had before him.

Writing and Discussion Question

George selected the middle name of 'Washington.' What would you pick for your middle name if you could choose it yourself? Why?

Internet Connections

To view current suggested links relating to this chapter's lessons, see www.fiveinarow.com/connections.

Chapter 8

Parent Summary

George has finally received an acceptance letter from a university! Highland College wants George to come and be a student on their campus. He can sign up for classes in the fall. George is thrilled. He sells his laundry business equipment and raises enough money for the train trip to Highland.

When George finally arrives at Highland College, he goes to visit the head of the university. George shows the man the letter he received and is stunned by the response he gets. Highland College won't accept George after all. The man tells George they didn't know he was black. Highland College doesn't accept Negroes. George leaves in tears.

Instead of running back to the Seymours, George decides to work and save money. As he works, he meets a man who tells him of a new government plan in the west. If a man works on a piece of land and lives on it for five years, he can own it. It's called homesteading. George thinks this is a fine idea. A farm of his own! At 22 years of age, George moves to Western Kansas. Although he does the best he can, after two years, no crops are growing well. George gives up and moves back east.

What we will cover in this chapter:

History and Geography: Homestead Act of 1862

Issues of Human Relationships: Injustice—Feeling Judged

Issues of Human Relationships: Ingenuity—Creativity in Your Finances

Lesson Activities

History and Geography: Homestead Act of 1862

George hears about a plan whereby he can secure a large farm, in return for living on the land and working it for five years (page 45). In the end, George's farm isn't successful. The land is too dusty and dry for crops to grow well there. But wasn't the plan a good one? If a person didn't have much money, here was a way by which he could secure a piece of land himself and build a farm for his family.

George was just one of hundreds of thousands of Americans who took advantage of this idea. Like George, people living on farms under this plan were known as 'homesteaders.' The United States Congress, in May of 1862, passed a law called The Homestead Act.

The Homestead Act stated that anyone over 21 years of age, who was the head of a family and a citizen of the United States could find, live and work on a 160 acre plot of land. If, after five years, he was still living on the land and improving it (using it for cattle, farming or industry), then he owned it—free and clear! In other words, if a person was willing to work very hard and make something out of an open plot of land, then he should have the right to call it his own.

Hundreds of thousands of people moved west from 1862 to 1900, setting up homesteads and securing farms for their families. Even during the early 1900s homesteading was still being accomplished in Alaska. In 1976, the Homestead Act was terminated for all states except Alaska. In 1986, the Homestead Act was abolished altogether.

Issues of Human Relationships: Injustice—Feeling Judged

George was told by the head of Highland College that he was not wanted there—because of the color of his skin (page 44). What an injustice! Perhaps your student, like George, has dealt with discrimination. However, even people who haven't felt racial injustice can sympathize with the emotion. Has your student ever felt wrongly judged? People can be cruel and often judge others' entire worth by details such as his clothes, or his father's job, how much money he makes, or even how much he weighs.

Talk with your student about a time when perhaps you, yourself, have felt your worth brought into question. How did it make you feel? Were you able to ignore the comments or move past them? How?

Perhaps your student has been involved in a situation, or maybe he has made the mistake of treating someone else with injustice. Learning to treat others with respect is part of what helps others have respect for you. Encourage your student to think about how he can work on seeing beyond superficial differences in others and focus on the strengths of each person he meets.

Issues of Human Relationships: Ingenuity—Creativity in Your Finances

George knew he would need money for a train ticket (page 43). How could he secure the funds? George decided to sell some of his belongings (a laundry tub, iron and ironing board). George used common sense and some ingenuity to raise the money. Learning to make money and to save some of it are things even young children can begin to understand.

Give your student a hypothetical situation. For example, pretend (or don't, if there is a real circumstance which is similar) that he wants a new bicycle for the summer. He decided in January on the bike he wants and it costs $120. He has until May (five months) to pay for the bike. What could he do to make money? Mow lawns? Help clean the house? Babysit? How much money, on average, would he make at each job? How quickly would those dollars add up?

Another topic of discussion is learning to save money. Being able to budget accurately, stick to a plan and realize your goal is a vital part of becoming mature. Does your student get an allowance? Does he have a budget? What things are included in the savings portion of his budget?

Learning to be creative and think of new ways to make money, and then having the maturity to save and spend wisely are all things your student can be learning and practicing while still young. George had an excellent head on his shoulders when it came to budgeting and money-making. He didn't have many opportunities when he was young, but he made the most of what he had. We can all learn a lesson from George!

Writing and Discussion Question

George was extremely excited at the prospect of attending Highland College. When he was told he would not be welcome there, George cried. Have you ever been excited about something and then felt sad when circumstances prevented it from happening? Write about a time when you felt as George felt and what you did to overcome the disappointment.

Internet Connections

To view current suggested links relating to this chapter's lessons, see www.fiveinarow.com/connections.

Chapter 9

Parent Summary

George travels for three months, heading east and north. He does odd jobs and laundry and soon finds himself in the town of Winterset, Iowa. In Winterset, George is hired as a cook at the Schultz Hotel. One day, a man at George's church introduces himself as Dr. John Milholland. George and the Milhollands become good friends. They help him open his own laundry business. Now George has work each day, but he is still actively learning new things about plants and flowers. Mrs. Milholland thinks George definitely belongs in college. The doctor tells George about Simpson College. George finds he can be accepted as a student even though he is black. So, on September 9, 1890, George is in college for the first time. He is much older than the other students, but delighted to be there!

What we will cover in this chapter:

History and Geography: Iowa—A New Place for George

Issues of Human Relationships: Self-Directed Study—Being Your Own Teacher

Career Path: Illustrator

Lesson Activities

History and Geography: Iowa—A New Place for George

George Washington Carver has been in many cities in Kansas and Missouri. This chapter, however, introduces yet another state—Iowa (page 47). If your student is interested, take some time and flip ahead in Eva Moore's book to page 53. There is a picture of the three-state area. Your student might wish to make his own representation of this map and mark the various towns George has been in thus far.

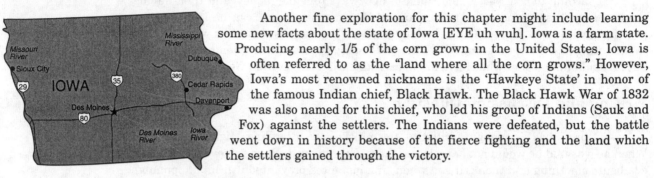

Another fine exploration for this chapter might include learning some new facts about the state of Iowa [EYE uh wuh]. Iowa is a farm state. Producing nearly 1/5 of the corn grown in the United States, Iowa is often referred to as the "land where all the corn grows." However, Iowa's most renowned nickname is the 'Hawkeye State' in honor of the famous Indian chief, Black Hawk. The Black Hawk War of 1832 was also named for this chief, who led his group of Indians (Sauk and Fox) against the settlers. The Indians were defeated, but the battle went down in history because of the fierce fighting and the land which the settlers gained through the victory.

There are states with many first generation foreign immigrants such as New York and California. However, Iowa has a population born primarily in the United States. In fact, a stunning 98% of all Iowans have been born in America.

Many famous Americans have been born in Iowa, including President Herbert Hoover, Carrie Chapman Catt (leader in the women's suffrage movement), and Norman E. Borlaug (winner of the 1970 Nobel Peace Prize).

Iowa is a rich and fertile state. Nearly 92% of the state's land is used as farmland—only the state of Nebraska has a higher percentage of farmland. Although the chief crop is corn, Iowa also produces soybeans and processes many pork products.

If your student is interested in learning more about Iowa, he can search the Internet for sites and his local library for more books on this traditionally *all-American* state.

Issues of Human Relationships: Self-Directed Study—Being Your Own Teacher

Draw your student's attention to page 49. Mrs. Milholland says that George is running his 'own school.' She tells people that "he is the teacher, and the pupil too." What does that mean to your student? Can a person be their own teacher? Absolutely! Sometimes, self-directed study can be the most beneficial and inspiring learning method in the world. Can *anyone* be their own teacher? Of course! Certainly, all children should be taught by educators or parents in a more formal setting for the majority of their school career. But any child can find a subject that fascinates him and begin to educate himself.

What is a subject your student finds particularly interesting? Is it something he could get a book about at the library? Does he know someone he could talk with who knows more about it? What about documentaries or films on the subject?

Encourage your student to follow George's example. If George, a financially struggling, young, black man in the late 1800s, was able to find sources for learning and form a self-directed study, then surely your student will be able to do even more!

Career Path: Illustrator

On page 48, we're told again how much George loves to paint. The young boy enjoys painting pictures of the flowers he is studying. Is your student interested in art? Does he find himself drawing and painting just for fun? Perhaps a career as an illustrator is something he should explore.

When someone says, "I'm an illustrator," we often think of the person who draws the pictures in books, primarily children's books. However, the area of illustration is much broader in scope than that. What about those pictures of plants and cells in a science textbook? Who draws the designs and beautiful covers on greeting cards? What person carefully sketches the representations of people and homes on the pamphlets used in community awareness outreach programs? The possibilities for an illustrator and his work are endless—including technical books, science/medical books, architectural plans, children's books, adult fiction, science fiction and many more.

Many illustrators use traditional mediums (i.e., watercolor, chalk, pencil/pens, paints, etc.) to create beautiful artwork. However, a growing trend is for illustration work to be completed by computer graphics. By using complex graphic art programs, artists are able to easily try hundreds of color combinations and look at many variations of the same piece of work. With each point of the drawing represented digitally on the screen, illustrators have complete control. Although some artists wouldn't enjoy using a computer as their medium, it has become a viable tool for many creators, who are called graphic artists.

Because the employment and career options are so varied in the area of illustration, college degree requirements also differ. However, your student can plan on needing a minimum of a Bachelor of Arts degree in illustration or drawing, and then possibly one to two more years of graduate work in a specified area of art.

For more information, contact an area college or university and ask for information on their art programs. Illustrating, whether books or technical materials, is a rewarding and delightful way to earn a living. Would your student like to see one of his pictures in a book someday?

Writing and Discussion Question

What is a topic you would like to pursue in a self-directed study? Do you have an area of interest you are already learning about on your own? Describe it.

Internet Connections

To view current suggested links relating to this chapter's lessons, see www.fiveinarow.com/connections.

Chapters 10 and 11

Parent Summary

George enjoys attending Simpson College. He makes a lot of friends and begins teaching others about his beloved plants and flowers. George continues to paint, but soon realizes that the life of an artist is too unstable. He also understands that the country isn't yet ready to accept a black artist. Instead, with the help of his teacher Miss Budd, he decides to pursue a degree in science and agriculture. George soon transfers to Iowa State College and begins to learn about farming and how crops grow.

In just a few years, George has learned a great deal about science—he has even written a booklet on plant diseases. People begin to talk about George Washington Carver and how brilliant he is. One particular person who hears about George is Booker T. Washington. Booker was the head of a college for black people in Alabama, called Tuskegee Normal School. Booker invites George to come and teach at Tuskegee. George accepts the offer. Soon he will be the director of the Agriculture Department! George Washington Carver is becoming very well known!

What we will cover in these chapters:

History and Geography: Tuskegee Normal School

History and Geography: Booker T. Washington

Science: Learning More about Birds

Fine Arts: Finger Painting—Being Messy Creatively

Lesson Activities

History and Geography: Tuskegee Normal School

On page 60, we learn George has been invited to teach at Tuskegee Normal School in Alabama. What an honor! Has your student ever heard of Tuskegee University (the current name for the institution)? Take some time to review a quick history of this famous place of learning.

Founded in 1881, by Booker T. Washington, Tuskegee University was a private school specifically set up for the education of black Americans. George Washington Carver is the school's best-known instructor. With a strong emphasis on agriculture and the sciences, Tuskegee is still a successful and active college campus today. The school offers courses in agriculture, home economics, business, education, engineering and architecture, nursing and veterinary medicine.

Included on the campus today is the George Washington Carver Museum, which can be toured and visited. This historic site, which includes the museum, was established in 1974 by Congress.

History and Geography: Booker T. Washington

Booker T. Washington invited George to come and teach at Tuskegee Normal School (page 60). Washington had heard of George and his amazing work with plants and crops at Iowa State. Does your student know anything about Booker T. Washington?

Beyond being the founder and director of Tuskegee University, Washington was the most influential black leader of his day. Advising two presidents (Theodore Roosevelt and Taft) on racial issues, writing an autobiography (*Up From Slavery* in 1901), founding the National Negro Business League and supporting a variety of black-owned newspapers helped B. T. Washington to have a dramatic impact on American culture and history.

However, not everyone appreciated or believed in the work Washington was doing for the black community. Other civil rights leaders began to attack and criticize the way in which Washington was fighting for his beliefs. The chief critic was historian and writer W. E. B. Du Bois. Du Bois believed that blacks should be allowed to attend all universities and colleges. He didn't appreciate Tuskegee limiting black students to agriculture and technical degrees. Du Bois wished that blacks would have more opportunities for higher education in all subjects, not just agricultural and industrial.

Washington gave a speech in Atlanta, Georgia in 1895 which set off sparks in many arenas of civil rights. He said, "In all things that are purely social we can be as separate as the fingers, yet as one as the hand in all things essential to mutual progress." Du Bois and others found this statement infuriating and dangerous. They were joined together to fight for complete equality, and did not wish to settle for segregation at any level.

By 1910, Du Bois and other leaders began new movements and the 'reign' of Booker T. Washington's ideas began to diminish.

Despite the differences in opinions about his work and life by others in the community, Washington did a great deal of good for black Americans. He certainly provided a platform for George Washington Carver to share his ideas and do good for others. Take this opportunity to research and report on Booker T. Washington and Du Bois and their surrounding histories.

Science: Learning More about Birds

On page 51, George is teaching his friends about birds and birds' songs. Is your student interested in birds? Does he enjoy watching the nesting process in the spring and the new baby hatchlings? Does he ever wonder which birds have blue eggs and which have brown eggs with spots? Has he ever heard a bird singing in a tree and wondered where it was and what it looked like? All of these questions are different ways that people can learn to identify birds. Bird watching is a highly popular hobby. Learning about birds is a complex science, known as *ornithology*.

Birds are fascinating creatures. They are beautiful, colorful, smart, and can fly! They build functional nests and homes for their young. A bird may migrate each year if need be, to stay in the weather conditions they require. Birds are graceful and lovely, but some can be fierce hunters as well. Did your student know that birds helped with the development of the first successful airplanes? Absolutely! Scientists and developers weren't able to make aircraft work until they studied the birds' wing and fashioned the airplane wings in a similar manner.

There are nearly 10,000 kinds of birds, ranging from the hummingbird (2 inches in length) to the ostrich (nearly 8 feet tall). There are birds in the tropics, the arctic, the desert and the mountains. Each bird is adapted to live well in his own climate. The bee hummingbird weighs only 1/28th of an ounce, while the emperor penguin can weigh over 300 lbs.!

Birds help us in a variety of ways. They provide many balancing effects for the environment. For example, hummingbirds feed on the nectar of flowers. As they move from flower to flower, just as bees do, they pollinate the blossoms. Another bird, the bobwhite, feeds on seeds. One bobwhite may help a farmer rid his fields of nearly 15,000 weed seeds daily. Hawks and other birds of prey assist farmers by eating mice and rats, animals that can ruin stored grain. Fruit-eating birds help spread seed by eating berries. The skin, pulp and nutrients are absorbed by the bird, but the viable seeds pass through their system and are dropped. Of course, as a direct source of food for humans, birds can be eaten. Ducks, turkeys, chickens, pigeons, quail, and other birds are often hunted or raised by and consumed by people.

If your student is interested in learning to identify birds, he can use many pieces of 'bird' information to assist him in his research. Each type of bird has a different type of feather, body shape, egg, beak, song and nest. First, he may enjoy identifying all the birds common in his neighborhood. Known as 'urban-dwellers,' these birds are often wrens, robins, blue jays, titmice, starlings, and sparrows. However, each area of the United States has specific birds, which are common to their region. What birds are in your student's backyard? Can he identify them by sight? By song? Has he looked them up in a book and noticed what their nests and eggs look like? Here is a topic that your student can research on his own and have a wonderful time learning. By drawing pictures or gathering found feathers, your student can compile his own notebooks or art books of all the birds he learns about. Use this opportunity to explore birds as an important part of your Science curriculum in this unit study!

Encourage your student to open his eyes and begin learning about the beauty and life of the birds around him!

Fine Arts: Finger Painting—Being Messy Creatively

Draw your student's attention to page 56. Our author tells us that when George was working on an art project he sometimes put down his brush and painted with his fingers! Did your student think that finger painting was just for little kids? Certainly not. Finger painting is a wonderfully messy and delightful way to create art—and adult artists sometimes use finger painting techniques as well!

If it has been awhile since your student has had the pleasure of creating a work of art with paints and his fingers, why not take this opportunity to let him try it again? If he holds two or three of his fingers together, or his whole fist squeezed together he can create different textures and designs in the paint. If he is feeling really daring, have him close his eyes and set a timer. When the timer goes off, have him open his eyes and see what he created by just feeling the paper and the paint.

Have a great time with this method of painting! If the teacher wants to join in the fun, by all means do so!

Writing and Discussion Question

George took better care of his health because he realized he had work he needed to do—people needed him. You're needed by your family and friends, too. What are things you can do to increase your health and take care of yourself?

Vocabulary Words

ornithology: the study of birds

W. E. B. Du Bois: black American leader, historian and sociologist (1868-1963)

Internet Connections

To view current suggested links relating to this chapter's lessons, see www.fiveinarow.com/connections.

Chapter 12

Parent Summary

George, settling into his new role at Tuskegee, begins by observing the local farmers and their fields. Astonished by the poor soil quality and the sagging crops, George decides to begin working on ways to increase the productivity of the farms. First, he must increase the richness of the soil by adding nitrogen back into the land. But before all of this, George decides he and his students need a building of their own on campus. By making their own bricks from clay, the students build an agriculture building. They set up a laboratory from things they find and scrap material that they collect. Soon they have their own "Experiment Station" set up as well. On this piece of land, they can set up "mock" farms and research what helps the soil and crops.

What we will cover in this chapter:

Science: Soil—What Role Nitrogen Plays

Science: Composting—What Is it?

Science: Legumes—What Are They?

Fine Arts: Making Bricks Out of Clay

Lesson Activities

Science: Soil—What Role Nitrogen Plays

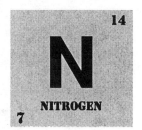

Dr. Carver and his students did experiments with nitrogen and soil in the Experiment Station (page 66). Nitrogen is essential for all living organisms—plants and animals. Nitrogen is a part of all amino acids—the base of all proteins. Plants can produce all the amino acids they need (thereby receiving their nitrogen), but animals (including people) must get the rest of these amino acids by eating other plants and/or animals.

In a cycle of chemical reactions called the nitrogen cycle, nitrogen is removed from the air, deposited into the earth and then returned to the air. Some plants, like legumes (cowpeas, beans, sweet peas and peanuts) grow in pods and give out nitrogen through their roots. When different plants are then grown in that same plot, the nitrogen remains in the soil and helps them grow. Later, the legume crops can be planted in that same plot again. This way of farming and gardening is called *crop rotation*.

Use this opportunity to learn more about nitrogen. Encourage and help your student to find library books appropriate for his age level on the nitrogen cycle, nitrates, nitrites and the greenhouse effect. You can also help your student search for this element on the Periodic Table of Elements. You can find this table listed in encyclopedias.

Science: Composting—What Is it?

On page 66, we see Dr. Carver encouraging his students to gather up garbage, grass clippings, manure and leaves and place them in a fenced-in pen. Then he tells them to add some soil from the woods and swamps and wait for it to rot. Is Dr. Carver crazy? Why would this help the farmland? What was he trying to accomplish?

Dr. Carver was teaching his students about composting. Has your student ever heard this term? Perhaps, if your student's family has a large garden, flowerbed or farm, then he has seen composting done before.

A compost pile is a collection of plant material, food waste products (vegetable skins, coffee grounds, etc.) and soil which is left to rot. As the materials break down and decay, nutrients become concentrated and provide rich nutrition for the soil.

Anyone can work on his own compost pile. If your student would like to try his hand at one, encourage him to set up a pen, similar to Dr. Carver's, somewhere outside. Even chicken wire can be formed into a small cylinder and stuck in the ground to make a great compost center. Now, have him begin collecting leaves, dirt and food scraps from the family. Remember—no meat products, but lots of vegetable matter. Old coffee grounds make a great addition! Encourage your student not to have a lot of any one addition, but instead to create a nice, even mixture of many things. He can sprinkle his compost pile with a little water to help speed up the decay process.

This experiment is best done in early spring and summer, since the heat of the sun helps break down the plant materials. When several weeks have gone by and your student's pile has rotted, he can try out his compost by planting some seeds in one pot, using only plain soil. Some more seeds can be planted in another pot using some soil *and* some compost. Which plants grow more quickly? Which are stronger?

Composting is an excellent way to grow bigger, better crops and recycle at the same time!

Science: Legumes—What Are they?

Dr. Carver encouraged his students to plant cowpeas, instead of cotton (page 66). He told them cowpeas are legumes and that they are good for the soil. Has your student ever heard the term 'legume' before? Take this opportunity to share a few essential 'legume' facts with your student.

Legumes [LEHG yooms] are all the plants that belong to the pea family—the second largest family of all flowering plants. Botanists have identified over 15,000 species of legumes! Legume species vary a great deal—from low shrubs to herbs and even trees! Delicious peanuts are legumes.

Legumes are good for the soil because they take in nitrogen from the air through their roots. Little nodules, or knot-like growths, form along the roots of the legumes. These nodules house bacteria, and this bacteria is what changes the nitrogen from the air to a valuable source of growth for the plant.

Because of the legumes and their way of infiltrating soil with nitrogen, many farmers plant legumes as cover crops and in crop rotation. If your student is interested in learning more about legumes, encourage him to find a book about peanuts, peas or the nitrogen cycle.

Fine Arts: Making Bricks Out of Clay

Dr. Carver's students worked hard to build their own agriculture building. By using the clay found in their area, they made bricks and built a functional two-story building for their classes.

Bricks are the oldest known man-made building material. In ancient times (by 6000 B.C.), sun-dried bricks were prevalent in the Middle East. By 3500 B.C., kiln-fired bricks were also being produced. Even today, in the American Southwest and in Mexico, sun-dried brick homes are still common. They are called adobe homes. Adobe [uh DOH bee] is the Spanish word for sun-dried brick. To make traditional adobe bricks, the workers mix sandy clay, a small amount of water and some straw or grass together. Then the mixture is placed in some sort of form (wooden or metal) and dried into bricks. When the clay is dry, the bricks are removed and laid in the sun for 10 days to 2 weeks. Then they can be used for building. Adobe homes are not practical for cold or rainy areas, because the sudden change in temperature or the wetness can compromise the integrity of the bricks and cause them to crumble.

Today, there are two main types of bricks commonly manufactured—building bricks and refractory bricks. Building bricks are extremely uniform in size and shape and are used to build walls, chimneys, houses, buildings, etc. Refractory bricks are made to handle very hot temperatures (2,000°-4,000° F.) and are used in factories, furnaces, and fireplaces. To make these bricks so heat resistant, they are often composed in part by materials such as alumina, carbon, and zircon.

If your student is finding this discussion of bricks interesting, why not let him try his own hand at building a few bricks? Even a mini-building? He can decide on the size of his bricks, how he will shape them and how many he will make. By using dirt, straw and water, he can make some very simple sun-dried bricks at home. If he wants to make a model or small structure that will hold up for a longer period of time, it might be wise to go to an art store and purchase some sculpting clay to mix with the dirt.

Then, get dirty and have fun! And remember how much work it must have taken for the students to build their agriculture classroom building!

Writing and Discussion Question

Dr. Carver told his students they didn't have any excuses (page 65). He said, "There's no need to whine, 'Oh, if I only had so-and-so!' Do it anyhow. Use what you find around you." Has there been a time you were forced to be inventive and use what you had around you? What did you do? How did it turn out? Have fun recalling and writing an explanation of your creativeness.

Vocabulary Words

legume: any plant belonging to the pea family

refractory brick: a brick used in high-temperature areas, such as furnaces and fireplaces

building brick: a brick made to be uniform and attractive and used for building outdoor exterior walls and homes

composting: a process by which plant material is broken down and decayed to produce high nutrient material for gardening and farming

Internet Connections

To view current suggested links relating to this chapter's lessons, see www.fiveinarow.com/connections.

Chapter 13

Parent Summary

Dr. Carver was happy in his role as professor and was much loved by his students. Everyone liked his gentle manner, intelligent teaching style and silly humor. Beyond teaching his students, Dr. Carver began to hold monthly meetings for the farmers in his area. By teaching them about their land and plants, Dr. Carver was teaching them how to be more successful farmers! Sometimes, Dr. Carver also led the group of farmers in prayer and song. He taught them how to sew and cook as well. Dr. Carver was busy helping everyone build stronger lives, better families and more prosperous farms.

What we will cover in this chapter:

Science: Insects—Identify Three New Insects Today

Language Arts: Humbug—A Literary Reference

Issues of Human Relationships:
Dealing with Practical Jokes—Learning to Laugh at Yourself

Career Path: Teacher

Lesson Activities

Science: Insects—Identify Three New Insects Today

Dr. Carver wanted his students to learn the names of every plant and insect they saw (page 68). What a wonderful goal Dr. Carver had for students. He wanted everyone to know as much about nature as they could. By following his example, encourage your student to take a moment and look through an encyclopedia or reference book and learn about three new insects today. What insect looks humorous? Which insect looks frightening? Is there a butterfly or type of ant that has always interested your student?

By drawing or coloring a picture of each of the three choices, writing down a few facts and telling you about his discoveries, your student can broaden his knowledge of the outside world today—just as Dr. Carver's students did each and every day. This might be a good opportunity to visit the library and find an age appropriate book on the insect world for your student.

If your student wants a few suggestions for insects to research, here are a few ideas: cicada killer, katydid, bagworms, silverfish and the spittlebug.

Language Arts: Humbug—A Literary Reference

Dr. Carver's students play a trick on him by combining parts of several insects to make a 'rare' bug (page 69). Dr. Carver calls it a 'humbug.' Does your student understand his joke? What does 'humbug' mean? A humbug is someone who pretends to be something he is not—a fake. Perhaps the most famous association with this term is found in Charles Dickens' masterpiece *A Christmas Carol*.

Ebenezer Scrooge, the main character in the delightful drama, doesn't believe in the Christmas spirit or in charity at all. Often in response to those who are much more cheery than he, he will respond, "Bah, Humbug." If your student or family has not shared this story before, do so now! It a wonderful tale anytime—not just at Christmas. As the changed Scrooge says in the end, "I will honour Christmas in my heart and try to keep it all the year."

Issues of Human Relationships:
Dealing with Practical Jokes—Learning to Laugh at Yourself

Dr. Carver's students played a joke on him by pretending to find a very unusual bug (page 68). Instead of getting embarrassed or upset with the teasing, Dr. Carver laughed it off and made his own joke. Has your student ever had a trick played on him? Has he ever been the brunt of a practical joke? Sometimes in life, people will tease us and instead of becoming frustrated or angry, it is best to learn to laugh at ourselves, and shrug off the teasing.

Learning to deal with other people and new situations is what growing up is all about. Encourage your student to laugh and join in the next time he is tricked or teased. It is the most fun and mature way to deal with those situations.

Career Path: Teacher

Dr. Carver was a wonderful teacher. He made his subject interesting, encouraged his students to strive for excellence and never quit learning himself. Has your student ever thought about becoming a teacher? Teachers are a respected and vital segment of our workforce today. Educating and training the children of our country is a large responsibility.

If your student is interested in looking into education as a career choice, remind him there are several basic requirements. First, does he enjoy learning? The best educators are people who love to learn themselves. Second, does your student enjoy passing information on to others patiently? These are two essential ingredients to being a successful teacher.

Teachers can be found in nursery care, preschools, grade schools, high schools, colleges and universities, vo-tech and training programs, specialized learning centers, boarding schools, after school programs for children, and many more places! To become a teacher, a four-year college degree and either graduate work or certification are almost always required. Teachers can be certified for specific grades, specific subjects, children with special needs, or all of the above. Hundreds of universities include a school of education and teaching certification programs.

If your student enjoys learning and sharing his knowledge with others, becoming a teacher might be a wonderful career path to explore. For more information, contact your local university or library for brochures, books, and resource materials. If your student knows a teacher, perhaps a visit to his or her classroom for observation might be helpful. Your student can take notes on what he sees and then write a paper on his discoveries. Did he enjoy a 'day in the life of a teacher?'

Writing and Discussion Question

Dr. Carver helped teach farmers how to grow better gardens. He encouraged his students and friends to plant legumes. If you could select the flowers and vegetables for your own garden, what would they be and why?

Internet Connections

To view current suggested links relating to this chapter's lessons, see www.fiveinarow.com/connections.

Chapter 14

Parent Summary

Dr. Carver and his students continue to research better ways to grow crops. They begin to plant sweet potatoes and soon discover what a simple and delicious crop they are! Dr. Carver wants to share his knowledge with even more farmers, so he begins to write pamphlets on his discoveries. For the farmers who can't read, Dr. Carver begins to travel and shows them what he has learned. Beyond growing sweet potatoes, Dr. Carver shows his friends and the farmers how to make beautiful yellow house paint from the Alabama clay. He also teaches the women how to make rugs and mats for their homes from dried okra stalks. In 1906, Tuskegee helps build a wonderful little school on wheels to take all the information around to area farmers. Dr. Carver is so happy he is now able to help even more people.

What we will cover in this chapter:

History and Geography: Dr. Carver's Pamphlets

Science: Sweet Potatoes

Lesson Activities

History and Geography: Dr. Carver's Pamphlets

On page 72 we read Dr. Carver began writing pamphlets about his experiences with sweet potatoes. The Tuskegee Institute began to print them and distribute them to farmers in the area. In this way, many more people could benefit from his findings.

In one such pamphlet, entitled *How The Farmer Can Save His Sweet Potatoes— And Ways of Preparing Them For The Table*, Dr. Carver covered such topics as the history of the sweet potato, its origins, the varieties available, how to grow them most effectively and how to cook them most deliciously. The recipes he discovered ranged from baking, frying, pies, glazes, cobblers, doughnuts, croquettes and even breads.

[**Teacher's Note**: Look at the following Fine Arts lesson for a few of the recipes taken from Dr. Carver's findings. Your student can whip up a delicious concoction and know he is making a dish Dr. Carver himself tried.]

Today, your student can still see these pamphlets in identically reproduced booklets. Available from the George Washington Carver Birthplace District Association located in Diamond, Missouri, your student can call for more information (417) 325-4151. There are pamphlet reproductions for the sweet potato and peanut available at nominal costs.

Science: Sweet Potatoes

Sweet potatoes became a passion for Dr. Carver. Share with your student some more scientific information about sweet potatoes to help enrich his understanding of our story.

Sweet potatoes are actually the edible roots of a plant, which belongs to the morning-glory family, *Convolvulaceae*. The roots of this plant are bulbous and fleshy, and are the section of the plant we harvest and consume. Originally believed to have been grown in South America, China now produces 85% of the world's sweet potatoes. Although the most common color of sweet potato flesh is yellow or orange, there are varieties that offer flesh from purple to white.

Remind your student that although many people confuse sweet potatoes with yams, they are two very different plants. Yams are mostly grown in the tropics, are a vine-type plant, and belong to the *Dioscoreaceae* family. Some yams can grow as large as 100 pounds!

Sweet potatoes are high in carbohydrates and in vitamins A and C. They are good for you, as well as delicious! Dr. Carver was right!

Language Arts: Folios and Pamphlets—Creating Your Own

Dr. Carver was able to spread his ideas and discoveries about sweet potatoes, farming, peanuts and more to a lot of people through the publication of pamphlets. Has your student ever done a research project or learned something exciting and wanted to share it? Take this learning opportunity to teach your student a bit more about the way books and pamphlets are constructed and then help him make one of his own.

Begin by examining a book together with your student. Try to locate a hardback, spined book, so your student can observe the sewn sections (called folios [FOH lee ohs]) which make up the book's pages. More expensive books are sewn onto canvas, and less expensive books are often made up of folios, which have simply been glued. Find an old book (perhaps you can pick one up from a garage sale or used-book sale) in which you are no longer interested or which is already extremely worn. As an interesting and helpful exercise, let your student take it apart and examine each section. Even-numbered pages, your student will notice, are always on the left, and odd-numbered pages are always located on the right.

Find a pamphlet or booklet and remove the staples or glue. Now allow your student to examine how each page is actually several. For example, the first piece of paper is both the back and front cover. The second piece of paper (laid on top) is the first page, second page, second to last page, and final page. Magazines are constructed the same way.

Once your student understands the basic concept of constructing a pamphlet, encourage him to create his own on whatever topic interests him. Remind him that he'll need to plan each page carefully so when it is folded the pages appear in the proper order. It might be helpful to compile the number of papers he wishes his pamphlet to contain first, and fold them like a book. Now he can see what pages will show in what order.

When his copy (the written portion) and his illustrations are completed, he can either staple or sew his "binding" together. Be sure to let your student show off his completed booklet to friends and family!

[**Teacher's Note**: A *wonderful* reference for this project is Valerie Bendt's *Creating Books With Children* ISBN 18880892-22-7. It is a resource you can use for many years.]

Fine Arts: Cooking with Sweet Potatoes

Just like Dr. Carver, your student can experiment in the kitchen using the same recipes he developed and found to be delicious. The following recipes are from Dr. Carver's booklet *How The Farmer Can Save His Sweet Potatoes* (Copyright 1937, Tuskegee Institute Press, Fourth Edition). Of course, the most common and favorite method of cooking sweet potatoes is still just baked. Roll up your sleeves, slip an apron on, and 'experiment' in the kitchen with your student today!

Recipe No. 25, Baked With Apples (delicious)

Take four medium sized potatoes and the same number of apples. Wash, peel and cut the potatoes in slices about 1/4" thick; pare and slice the apples in the same way; put in baking dish in alternate layers; sprinkle 1 1/2 cups of sugar over the top, scatter 1/2 cup of butter over the top; add 3/4 pint of hot water; bake slowly for one hour; serve steaming hot.

Recipe No. 18, Croquettes

Take two cups of mashed, boiled, steamed or baked sweet potatoes; add the beaten yolks of two eggs and season with salt and pepper to taste; stir over the fire until the mass parts from the sides of the pan. When cold, form into small croquettes, roll in egg and breadcrumbs, and fry in hot oil to amber color. Serve on napkins.

Sweet Potato Biscuits

Take:
1/2 cup mashed sweet potatoes
1/2 tsp. salt
1 cup flour
4 tsp. baking powder
2 Tbs. butter or lard
milk sufficient to make soft dough

Mix your dry ingredients together and then begin adding the potatoes in small batches, mixing with knife. Work the butter into the mixture with knife. Now begin adding milk, until soft dough is formed. Turn out onto floured board, pat and roll out, until 1/2" thick. Cut into biscuits; place on greased pans and bake 12 to 15 minutes at 400° F.

Issue of Human Relationships: Waste Not, Want Not

George Washington Carver believed in using what he saw around him. Wasting was simply not an option. Becoming more aware of what we waste and throw away is helpful in becoming better consumers. Does your student think his family throws away too many things? Food scraps? Paper scraps? Magazines? Old clothes? Plastic shampoo and soap bottles? Aluminum cans?

Encourage your student to think of at least five ways his family can recycle or reuse items on a routine basis to help cut down on wasteful living. For example, old clothing can always be given to homeless shelters or organizations like Good Will. If a sock has a hole in it, it could be mended and worn again instead of thrown away. Jeans with ripped out knees can be patched and worn as work or play pants or turned into a dusting mitt. Old newspapers can be rolled and formed into wonderful fire starter sticks. Many food scraps can be used in composting piles to create rich mulch for garden areas. Plastic products, aluminum cans, and bottles can all be easily collected and recycled at centers in your area. Old computer paper, the back of old school assignments and even junk mail can be cut into uniform squares on a paper cutter, and stapled into scratch note pads for use around the house.

How many more ways can your student come up with to help recycle and reuse items around his house? Learning to use what we have most effectively allows us to get more out of what we have. Using good stewardship can also benefit others and save our natural resources for future generations.

Writing and Discussion Question

Some of the farmers Dr. Carver spoke with about farming could not read. Do you think adult illiteracy is still a problem in the United States? Do some research and discuss your findings. What are some ways you think would be helpful in fighting adult illiteracy?

Internet Connections

To view current suggested links relating to this chapter's lessons, see www.fiveinarow.com/connections.

Chapter 15

Parent Summary

Dr. Carver has now been teaching at Tuskegee for over ten years. In 1909 a new agriculture building was built, and Dr. Carver and his students had a wonderful new laboratory to work in. Dr. Carver finally had so many speaking engagements, he was forced to give up teaching, but he still maintained relationships with his students. Sometimes he held special nature classes for very young children. His students and friends found him to be a sweet man who didn't care about his clothes or personal possessions. He just wanted to help people and teach them more about the world around them.

[**Teacher's Note**: Due to the brevity of this chapter, use this time to review any lessons you may have missed in the previous chapters. Also, review main topics and projects you may have discussed earlier.]

What we will cover in this chapter:

Science: Gardens and Flowers

Issues of Human Relationships: Owning A Pet—The Care and Commitment

Lesson Activities

Science: Gardens and Flowers

Dr. Carver thought each child should have a little garden of his own (page 76). Why does your student think he said this? Gardening can provide children with several key learning opportunities. First, it helps teach responsibility. It can stimulate interest in educational topics like horticulture, botany, the water cycle, heredity, nutrition, art, etc. Does your student have a little garden of his own? Would he like to make one? Even in a window box or pot, a child can create a flower garden, an herb garden, or even have a tomato or pepper plant.

Gardening is a wonderful hobby. It provides exercise, keeps you in contact with the outdoors and can be very relaxing. It can also be rewarding if you are able to eat your crop!

If your student is interested, encourage him to locate some books on gardening from his local library to learn more about what is involved—watering, fertilizer, soil erosion, growing regions, plant varieties, pesticides, insects, weeding, harvesting, flower cutting, etc. If he is able, perhaps he would like to plant a garden of his own and give it a try. No matter how successful it is, Dr. Carver would have been proud!

Issues of Human Relationships: Owning A Pet—The Care and Commitment

George Washington Carver believed that all children should be able to care for small animals (page 76). Does your student have a pet? Does he want one? Perhaps if there is an animal your student is highly interested in (or one he has always wanted to have for a pet) he can do research on all the things required for that pet. For example, lizards need heat lamps, sometimes live food, rocks, glass tanks and fearless masters. Parakeets require seed, cage, toys, grit, beak bones, papers changed each day, and an attentive owner.

Owning a pet is a great deal of fun, but it also demands a high level of commitment. Being responsible for an animal is perhaps the first way many people learn certain aspects of parenthood. If a puppy is that much work, imagine how much work a human baby would be!

When your student has done his research on a particular pet, encourage him to either write a paper or give an oral report. He can create posters and visual aids on his topic and present it to siblings, parents or friends.

Writing and Discussion Question

Dr. Carver tells his young friend on page 77, "Now take it back and turn it loose, my boy. Take it back to its mother. It is terrible when a young bird is taken from its mother." Why do you think Dr. Carver said this? Why was he upset by the baby bird being taken from its mother? What personal attachments might he have to this scenario?

[**Teacher's Note**: This question requires your student to recall biographical information about Carver's early life and how it related to the baby bird incident. Recalling and synthesizing information to form conclusions is an important academic and life skill.]

Internet Connections

To view current suggested links relating to this chapter's lessons, see www.fiveinarow.com/connections.

Chapters 16 and 17

Parent Summary

Dr. Carver continues to work on his experiments with the sweet potato, and then begins working with peanuts as well. He develops scores of uses for each plant and is soon being called "The Wizard of Tuskegee." Famous people like Thomas Alva Edison begin to approach Dr. Carver. They want him to come work with them, but he chooses to stay at Tuskegee. Dr. Carver wants to help support his black friends and give back to them his knowledge and training.

What we will cover in these chapters:

History and Geography: Royal Society

History and Geography: Martin Luther King, Jr.— "I Have A Dream"

Science: Sweet Potatoes and Peanuts—The Uses and Products of Dr. Carver

Lesson Activities

History and Geography: Royal Society

Dr. Carver's experiments were so profound and exciting he was invited to join an elite group of scientists through an organization called The Royal Society of Arts (page 81). Is this prestigious group still in existence? Yes. In fact, it has been around for a very long time.

Now called The Royal Society of London for Improving Natural Knowledge (or just 'The Royal Society'), this group is the world's oldest known existing scientific organization. Founded in 1660, the Royal Society is devoted to development and recognition of scientists in areas such as biology, chemistry and mathematics. Interesting to note, the

Royal Society has over 1,000 members worldwide. Its offices in London house over 120,000 books and 200,000 manuscripts!

History and Geography:
Martin Luther King, Jr.— "I Have A Dream"

Draw your student's attention to page 86. Why does the guard ask Dr. Carver to leave the city park? If you have already discussed racial segregation with your student in lessons from past chapters, take this opportunity to enrich his understanding with a look at Martin Luther King, Jr., and his famous speech on August 28, 1963, during the March On Washington.

[Teacher's Note: If your student has not covered racial segregation yet, you may wish to take a few moments and refer to the index for past lessons on this subject in this volume.]

In response to the guard's request, Dr. Carver says quietly to himself, "They don't understand." Another man, famous in our history, said similar words to himself on many occasions. Dr. Martin Luther King, Jr., was a black activist who worked tirelessly for the end to segregation and an overall improvement in race relations in the United States.

Born in Atlanta, Georgia, in January of 1929, young Martin Luther King's father was a minister in a Baptist church. In school the boy excelled and soon graduated from high school at fifteen. Entering Morehouse College at that same age, Martin decided to become a minister just like his father and grandfather. In 1953 King married Coretta Scott. By 1955 at the age of 26, King had obtained a bachelor's degree, a Divinity degree, and a Ph.D. in Theology.

King began his interest in civil rights in 1955 during and after the Montgomery bus system protest and Rosa Parks' stand for justice.

[Teacher's Note: If you are able, this is an excellent time to have some discussions with your student about Rosa Parks and the amazing role she played in the civil rights movement. You'll find a variety of children's books and short biographies on Rosa Parks at the library.]

King, urged by fellow black activists, began giving speeches on his beliefs regarding civil rights and the problems America faced. Unlike some of his colleagues, however, King insisted on non-violent protests.

Although he had many successful boycotts, sit-ins and speeches, perhaps no moment more clearly defines the Civil Rights movement or King's life than his speech given on August 28, 1963, at a massive march in Washington, D.C. On that day, over 200,000 Americans (including many white people) crowded around the Lincoln Memorial. In his speech, entitled "I Have A Dream," Martin Luther King, Jr., spoke of his hope for our nation. You might want to examine the full text of Dr. King's speech, but you can begin by discussing these two simple thoughts from the speech:

"I have a dream that one day this nation will rise up and live out the true meaning of its creed: 'We hold these truths to be self-evident: that all men are created equal.' I have a dream that one day on the red hills of Georgia the sons of former slaves and the sons of former slaveowners will be able to sit down together at a table of brotherhood."

On April 4, 1968, while in Memphis, Tennessee, Dr. Martin Luther King, Jr., was shot and killed by a white escaped convict, James Earl Ray. On King's tombstone are the words, "Free at last, free at last, thank God Almighty, I'm free at last."

If your student is interested and you live in the area, a wonderful museum to tour is the National Civil Rights Museum located in Memphis at the site of King's assassination. Also, draw your student's attention to the third Monday in January each year—Martin Luther King, Jr., Day. It is a federal holiday honoring King, his life and his work for each of us. The holiday was passed by Congress in 1983.

Science:
Sweet Potatoes and Peanuts—The Uses and Products of Dr. Carver

Dr. Carver developed over 300 uses for the peanut and over 100 uses for the sweet potato. Have your student try to guess what types of products these were and then show him the following lists and see if he is surprised by the diversity. Remind your student of Dr. Carver's favorite adage, "Waste not, want not."

Peanuts

margarine	salad oil	illuminating oil
massage oil	soap	medicines
glycerin	cosmetics	bedding for livestock
explosives	insulation	sweeping compounds
paper board	fertilizer	artificial wool
plastic filler		

Sweet Potatoes

synthetic rubber	tapioca	postage stamp glue
molasses	dyes	coffee
starch	flour	

Writing and Discussion Questions

Why do you think Dr. Carver "holed" himself away in his laboratory by the hour? What purpose could that serve? If you were conducting experiments, would you act the same way? Why or why not?

Dr. Carver made an entire meal out of peanuts, each different dish being made from the versatile legume. Describe how you think that would taste. Would you like to try a meal like that? Why or why not?

Internet Connections

To view current suggested links relating to this chapter's lessons, see www.fiveinarow.com/connections.

Chapters 18 and 19

Parent Summary

Dr. Carver spends more and more time giving speeches all around the world. Wherever he goes, all the seats are filled. He never gets married, but instead lives alone, doing his experiments and research projects. At age 72, in 1936, Dr. Carver still lives at Tuskegee in his two-room dorm and has been at the college for 40 years. The college hires an artist to make a statue of Dr. Carver for the anniversary celebration. And in 1948, the United States Post Office honors Dr. Carver with a commemorative stamp with his picture on it.

For the next few years Dr. Carver works as much as he can on plans for the George Washington Carver Museum located at Tuskegee. He meets President Franklin D. Roosevelt while working on this project and receives a special medal for his service.

In 1941 the museum opens and Dr. Carver is there for the ceremony. Early in the morning on January 5, 1943, George Washington Carver dies at age 79. He lived a life of service.

What we will cover in these chapters:

Science: Synthetics—What They Are and How They Help Us

Fine Arts: Crayons and Carver

Issues of Human Relationships:
Living a Life of Service—Developing a Servant's Heart

Lesson Activities

Science: Synthetics—What They Are and How They Help Us

Your student may have noticed a word he is unfamiliar with on page 92—synthetics. Dr. Carver worked on what is now known as synthetic chemistry. Synthetic chemists work on developing new substances or compounds from two or more elements. Synthetics are things like all plastics, Styrofoam, nylon, vinyl, plastic wrap, spandex, acetate, polyester and many more.

Take a look through your kitchen—plastic bowls, plastic spoons, plastic cups, plastic plates, soap bottles, etc., are all synthetic products. Can you imagine our world without plastics? And what about your student's tights? Or pajamas? Or bicycle? Or shoes? So many pieces of our daily life reflect the development and use of synthetics.

Chemists and manufacturers produce synthetics by combining elements such as carbon, nitrogen and oxygen in various quantities and under different conditions. As these compounds are formed, the chemical processes create different synthetics. The most common chemical process by which scientists can create synthetics is called polymerization. Polymerization involves converting small molecules into larger ones.

George Washington Carver was one of the first scientists in history to experiment with synthetics and realize their importance.

To help your student grasp how important synthetics have become in our daily lives, sit in a specific room and have him guess (without trying to count) how many synthetic items he thinks are around him. Then, with your help, start at one side of the room and begin listing each item he sees which is made using synthetics. You will both be amazed! Dr. Carver was truly a scientist ahead of his time! Find appropriate level books on synthetics in general or specific plastics at your local library and learn more!

Fine Arts: Crayons and Carver

Although our book does not include this aspect of Carver's discoveries, your student may be interested in knowing that he developed the early synthetic pigments and waxes used to make the first crayons—long before Crayola® jumped into the picture! How many young children, every day, eat a sandwich made with peanut butter (also invented by Carver) and color with crayons? Millions! Those two contributions alone have provided many children (and adults) with a great deal of enjoyment!

Why not take a break and enjoy a nice peanut butter sandwich in honor of Dr. Carver. And while you're at it, draw a picture with some crayons. Perhaps a portrait of the kind inventor himself, or whatever your student wishes. And while you're munching and drawing, be thankful for the wonderful spirit of creativity and servanthood Carver demonstrated through his life.

Issues of Human Relationships:
Living a Life of Service—Developing a Servant's Heart

When the young George Carver was first setting out on his own to Neosho to attend school, little did he know the path his life would take. Fame and fortune were certainly not his goals, but instead, to serve others and provide his fellow black brothers and sisters with tools which would enable them to help themselves. He was offered many working positions around the world from people as famous as Thomas Edison, Henry Ford and Josef Stalin. These men offered great sums of money and unlimited resources to Carver in exchange for his technical expertise and commitment. But Carver insisted on staying near his roots and serving at Tuskegee. Carver never married, and in 1940 he gave his life savings of $33,000 to the Tuskegee Institute. He asked that the funds be used to establish the George Washington Carver Research Foundation—dedicated to furthering agriculture research.

What does your student think of Carver's approach to life? Certainly not everyone is as devoted to a life of service as Carver, but we can all learn to develop more of a giving heart by looking to him as an example. What can your student do, even at his age, to help others and exhibit a servant's heart? By offering to help around the house, reading to an elderly person or grandparent, spending time with his siblings, purchasing a toy for an underprivileged child, helping out at a soup kitchen or shelter house, etc., each of us can find a few moments in our daily lives to help someone who is less fortunate. Encourage your student to think of Carver as an example of what we should each strive for in our lives.

Writing and Discussion Questions

Do you find it interesting that Dr. Carver refused the fame and fortune that so many offered him? Would you refuse such offers? Why? Why not?

Internet Connections

To view current suggested links relating to this chapter's lessons, see www.fiveinarow.com/connections.

SKYLARK
BY PATRICIA MacLACHLAN

Chapter 1

Parent Summary

This is the first chapter in the sequel to *Sarah, Plain and Tall*. Papa and Sarah are now married, and the four Wittings live together on the prairie.

Our first glimpse at the family is with them getting their photograph taken. Sarah wants to send a wedding/family picture back home to Maine. We also learn from their conversation with the photographer that the prairie is experiencing an intense drought. Some families have been forced to move. Papa tells Sarah and the children that they would never leave the prairie. He says, "We were born here. Our names are written in this land." Caleb and Anna agree but both wonder—what about Sarah? She wasn't born on the prairie. Her name isn't written in the land.

What we will cover in this chapter:

History and Geography: Family Portraits

History and Geography: A Look Back at the Dirty '30s

Science: Photography—An Overview

Language Arts: A Writer's Style—MacLachlan's Use of Nature

Language Arts: A Reading Recommendation: *Three Names*

Issues of Human Relationships: Avoiding Hurting Others When You Hurt

Lesson Activities:

History and Geography: Family Portraits

Joshua came to take the Wittings' wedding photo (page 3). Has your student ever had a family photograph taken? What was it like? Did the photographer meet the family somewhere (park, at their home, outside, etc.)? Did the family go to the studio? How did your student's family dress? Was the picture copied and sent to different family members?

In the late 19th century and early 20th century (the time of our story), photographs were a much larger production than they are today. Today we have 35 mm cameras for snapshots and many people carry one with them all the time—to the zoo, on vacation, etc. Pictures are very common. But back then, a photograph was a major event. For some families (like the Wittings), they may have only had one or two photographs taken of them in their entire lifetimes.

Sarah wanted a wedding picture (including Anna and Caleb—and Nick and Lottie) to send back to Maine for her Aunts (page 4). Many pioneer families (in the west or out on the prairie) would save their money and hire a photographer to take a picture of them in order to send back to their relatives. But what if you lived on the prairie and wanted a picture of your family—could you get one taken that day? Probably not. Unless you were lucky enough to live in a town where a local photographer worked, you would have to wait until a photographer was traveling near your home and schedule the session then. Many people on the prairies may have only a few photographs ever taken of them!

It was common in those days, as well, for families to pull some of their prize possessions outside just for the photograph. At that time, flash photography wasn't possible, making interior photos difficult. The families wanted their relatives back home (generally in the east) to see that they were prosperous and doing well. A piano, a beautiful sofa, a prize Victrola, etc.—these things would be moved outside onto the lawn and the family would stand proudly next to their things.

Can your student imagine doing that today? Dragging the piano outside in order to take a photograph next to it?

Today, photographs are common. Perhaps your student even has a camera of his own. Families still schedule sittings for family photographs, but today the cost is much more reasonable and every town or city has dozens of studios. It is not the event it once was.

Perhaps, if your student is interested, it might be enjoyable to do a family photograph. If this is done with a serious note, studios can be contacted for prices or even stores (Wal-Mart, Sears, etc.) do very inexpensive family photos. If your student would like to "recreate" an "old-timey" family photo, encourage him to formulate in his mind how he would like it to look. Standing under a tree, perhaps with a few chairs (rocking chairs would be good) and someone holding a fancy clock, a family photograph from the late 19th century can be recreated. By using black and white film, his family can be photographed beautifully.

Or if your student has even more creativity for the project, an "updated" family photo can be taken with the family's current prize possessions pictured with them. Have each family member choose something which represents "1990s success" to them (examples: Dad—laptop computer or tools; Mom—cellular phone or modern kitchen mixer; child—new bicycle or card collection). Then take a "'90s" photograph with each family member next to, or holding their object.

This can be a great history lesson and planning project for your student. He can even mount the photo and write a little description beneath to hang in his room or in his home.

History and Geography: A Look Back at the Dirty '30s

The Wittings are experiencing a bad drought on the prairie (page 5). If your student has finished *Beyond Five in a Row*, Volume 1, refer back to the lesson on the Dirty '30s in chapter 2 of *The Boxcar Children*. A brief reminder of what they studied in that section will help enrich their understanding of *Skylark*. If you did not cover this lesson or did not use Volume 1, here is an excerpt from that lesson.

A tragic and scary time in American history occurred during the mid-1930s across the plains of Kansas, Oklahoma, Texas and the adjacent parts of Colorado and New Mexico. This area of the United States became known as the Dust Bowl. The name came from the low annual rainfall and high winds that blew dust and dirt for miles.

During the years 1934-1937, farmers in this area of the country had stripped the land of the natural grasses and planted fields of wheat. Without the aid of the root systems of the natural plants, too much dirt and dust was picked up by the high winds. Soon dust storms formed and buried entire houses. More than half the population was forced to leave the area. Our government replanted the grasses and trees and helped the land return to its natural state. Self-directed research on the Dust Bowl years can make an interesting project for students.

Science: Photography—An Overview

Taking a photograph is not difficult. Taking a fine photograph takes a lot of training and artistic planning. But has your student ever thought about what goes into the actual development of the film? How does a camera work? What is film made of? What happens to the film after you drop it off at the processing center? How is a picture really made?

If your student is interested in photography, take some time to introduce him to the five basic steps in the process of photography: (1) collecting light, (2) focusing, (3) exposing the film, (4) developing and (5) creating the printed picture.

Any one of these five areas of photography would make an excellent adventure for your student to study. Here, among many others, are a few of the questions your student can research:

What is an aperture? What is a latent image? How is silver used in the film process? What chemicals are used to create a print? Why can undeveloped film never be exposed to light? What is a darkroom? What shape is a camera lens?

Encourage your student, if interested, to take a trip to his local library (or begin with a glance through an encyclopedia) and see if he can answer some of these questions.

Photography fully incorporates both science (chemistry and calculations) and creativity (positions, compositions, subject selection, etc.).

Language Arts: A Writer's Style—MacLachlan's Use of Nature

Our author, Patricia MacLachlan, certainly has her own writing style. One of the things you can explore with your student is her use of three specific subjects in her chapters' opening lines. The three subjects are flowers/plants, animals and seasons. For example, draw your student's attention to the first line of *Skylark*, "Papa married Sarah on a summer day."

If you refer back to *Sarah, Plain and Tall*, here are some chapter 'openers:'

Chapter 2 – *...and before the ice and snow had melted from the fields...*
Chapter 3 – *Sarah came in the spring.*
Chapter 4 – *The dogs loved Sarah first.*
Chapter 5 – *The sheep made Sarah smile.*
Chapter 6 – *The days grew longer...*
Chapter 7 – *The dandelions in the fields had gone by...*
Chapter 8 – *The rain came and passed...*

Your student, if he is observant, will find the same 'nature' motif used by MacLachlan in *Skylark*. Although not in every chapter, the majority of opening lines include the weather/seasons, animals or plants. Certainly, this is not what your student 'should always' do in his own writings. Every author chooses different styles for his writing. However, it is interesting to note for your student that as he writes his stories, he can be thinking of different 'motifs' to use himself. Perhaps each of his chapters might begin with someone talking or with one particular character's thoughts. Perhaps his chapters could include a description of a different feature of one character. There is a great variety of topics which would make an interesting 'through-line' for his writing. Your student's choice of motif will help carry the reader smoothly from chapter to chapter.

Language Arts: A Reading Recommendation: *Three Names*

If your student is enjoying this study of *Skylark*, perhaps it would be fun to read some other books by Patricia MacLachlan. This is the way many people find new, interesting books. If they enjoy one, they begin to search for other books by the same author. Interesting to note, many of MacLachlan's books also center around the prairie as their subject.

If your student went through the original *Five in a Row* series of books, perhaps he studied *Three Names* (located in Volume 2). Written by MacLachlan, *Three Names* (Copyright 1991) is the story of a young boy's great-grandfather, his dog and life on the prairie. It is an excellent study in description and even very young children can appreciate the sweet story.

If your student has already studied this book, you may wish to simply go back and reread it. If you have never read this story, locate a copy and share it with your student. Encourage him to compare the writing (description, style, dialogue) with MacLachlan's work in *Sarah* and *Skylark*.

Issues of Human Relationships: Avoiding Hurting Others When You Hurt

Explore with your student the interchange between Anna and Caleb toward the bottom of page 6. Both children are nervous about Sarah and Papa and the drought. As Caleb verbalizes, "Sarah wasn't born here." What if the drought forces them to leave? What if Sarah misses the green and rain of Maine?

Caleb decides to solve the problem in his own way. He will write Sarah's name in the land himself. We know, of course, it is just a figure of speech to have "one's name in the land." And Anna understands this too. But she is quick to criticize Caleb and is hurtful when she says, "You can't even spell Caleb. You can't." The book tells us that Anna was sorry for being cross, but she doesn't apologize to Caleb. Why do people sometimes lash out at others when they are frightened or hurt? Has your student ever hurt someone else's feelings when *he* was the one hurting? Does it really make you feel any better to hurt someone else?

Encourage your student to recognize when he is being 'short' with someone, and to monitor his own feelings. Is he simply taking it out on the other person because he is scared or hurting himself? Instead of needlessly hurting the other person, share with your student other ways to cope with his feelings.

If a person is brave, sharing with someone your concerns or fears can be greatly beneficial. But if the hurt is too deep or the fear too great, other activities can take your mind off of your problems (instead of lashing out at others). Exercising, walking, building a model, drawing a picture (perhaps a picture of yourself and how you're feeling), reading a book or just hammering on some wood are all good ways to relieve tension and not hurt someone else in the process.

Anna allowed her own fear and worry to hurt Caleb. She was wrong, but we can understand how she was feeling. Learning to direct our emotions in constructive and non-damaging ways is a sign of maturity and growth.

Writing and Discussion Question

How do you think Caleb felt when Anna told him he couldn't spell? Knowing Caleb's character, do you think he would have returned the mean comment with an equally mean reply? What do you think he might have said back to her?

Vocabulary Word

motif: a principle idea, motive or theme

Internet Connections

To view current suggested links relating to this chapter's lessons, see www.fiveinarow.com/connections.

Chapter 2

Parent Summary

The days grow hotter and hotter, and still no rain comes to the prairie. Papa tells Sarah she'll have to quit washing the floor, in order to save water. She thinks that is a mixed blessing. Other things are changing as well. Seal is pregnant and will have kittens. We also find out Anna is keeping a diary—notes on her life and Papa, Caleb and Sarah.

[**Teacher's Note**: If your student hasn't already noticed, this would be a good time to draw his attention to the italicized portions of writing at the end of each chapter. In this chapter, we find out that Anna keeps a diary. As you continue to read, it becomes obvious the italicized portions are excerpts from her journal. The story is written in first person, so we are already privy to Anna's thoughts and feelings. However, these journal entries give us an even more intimate look at how she perceives her world and her family—a nice addition by Patricia MacLachlan to the already delightful text.]

What we will cover in this chapter:

Science: Gestation Periods in Different Animals

Fine Arts: Watercolor Painting and Color Mixing

Lesson Activities

Science: Gestation Periods in Different Animals

Seal isn't just getting fat. She's pregnant (page 9)! Does your student know how long it takes for a cat to have kittens? What is that period of time called, while the baby is still in the mother? Is a cat's pregnancy time different from other animals? Take this opportunity to share some fascinating animal science information with your student, beginning with some general facts surrounding all animals.

Scientists have classified nearly one million kinds of animals. This amazing figure can be broken down into all the categories of animals, including more than 4,000 kinds of mammals.

A cat is a mammal. To be called a mammal, an animal must be warm-blooded, (generally) covered in hair, whose offspring (babies) are fed by milk from the mother. The period of time during which the baby(ies) are in the mother's womb is called by scientists, the period of gestation. For a human baby, the gestation period is nine months. A baby born earlier than that would be called premature. However, the gestation period differs from animal to animal. Here are a few examples of the variety:

Animal	Offspring	Gestation Period
Chicken	Chick	21 days
Cat	Kitten	2 months
Beaver	Pup	3 months
Bear	Cub	6-8 months
Cow	Calf	9 months
Horse	Foal	11 months
Giraffe	Calf	14-15 months
Whale	Calf	15-17 months
Elephant	Calf	18-23 months

Imagine a human having to be pregnant for as long as an elephant—nearly two years! Each animal's gestation period is just long enough for all the necessary developments to take place and for the young to be born healthy. See if your student can find which animal on the chart has the same gestation period as a human. Which animal is pregnant for nearly one year? And how long will it take for Seal's kittens to be born?

Fine Arts: Watercolor Painting and Color Mixing

On page 14, in Anna's journal entry, we read that Sarah teaches Anna how to paint with watercolors. Has your student ever tried this type of painting? Often referred to as 'transparent painting,' watercolor painting can be simple or complex, and very rewarding.

For just a couple of dollars, invest in a simple box of watercolors. Prang®, available at any discount store or art shop, does very well for beginners. A simple brush, a jar of water and some paper, and your student is set.

Watercolor painting can be quite satisfying. Allow your student to experiment with the different values of colors (a color value refers to the intensity of the shade—a blue can have a light value (sky blue) or a dark value (midnight blue)). Various shades can be achieved depending upon the ratio of water to paint on the brush. If the brush is more 'watery' then the value will be lighter. Brushing with very little water is called 'dry brushing.'

Watercolors can also be an excellent jumping off point for a discussion on color mixing. Most children, at this age, understand the term primary color. The three primary colors are red, yellow and blue. All other colors come from a combination of these three. Secondary (binary) colors are created by mixing two primaries. For example, orange is made from red and yellow. Green is made from yellow and blue. Purple is made from red and blue. Tertiary colors are created by blending a secondary and a primary—red-orange, blue-green, etc.

Two other terms useful for students are analogous [a NAL a gus] and complementary. Analogous colors are colors that are adjoining or adjacent to any one of the primaries on the color wheel and are obviously similar in nature. For example, red, red-orange and red-violet are analogous because they all contain red. Complementary colors are opposite in their origin (opposite each other on the color wheel)—blue and orange, red and green, yellow and violet.

To understand these concepts better, it is useful to create a color wheel with your student. Look in the Appendix for a color sheet with instructions on how to fill it out. Once your student has completed the sheet, he will better understand these concepts.

To practically apply this color lesson, share the following example with your student. If he is painting a picture of a house with sunlight on it, he will, no doubt, use yellow/orange shades to bathe his house in 'sun.' To make shadows, many artists would then choose purple or blue hues. Through the contrast of these complementary colors (yellow and blue), his 'sunny' areas will appear that much more brilliant.

As your student continues to experiment with watercolors and different hues, encourage him not to make a common art mistake by watering down or selecting dull colors. Timidity in young artists often results in this 'pale' effect. It is better to make strong color choices and learn which ones complement one another (or provide the most contrast), than to try to 'harmonize' everything and have a lifeless painting as a result. Your library will probably have several good books on color theory, if your student is interested.

Writing and Discussion Question

On page 11 Sarah tells Caleb and Anna that she loved what was "between the lines" in Papa's letters. What does that saying mean? How would you have described it to Caleb?

Vocabulary Words:

gestation: the act or process of the young developing in the uterus

premature: a baby who is born earlier than the full gestational period

primary colors: red, yellow and blue

secondary colors: colors created by blending primaries

tertiary colors: colors created by blending a primary and secondary

analogous: colors which are similar, close on the color wheel

complementary: colors which are opposite in origin

Internet Connections

To view current suggested links relating to this chapter's lessons, see www.fiveinarow.com/connections.

Chapter 3

Parent Summary

On Sunday, the Wittings go to church and talk with their friends about the drought. Still, no rain has come and everyone is worried. The next day, Anna is awakened by Caleb calling to her in a very excited voice. During the night, Mame, their cow, gave birth to her calf. Papa says the calf's face is as pale as the winter moon. Caleb names her Moonbeam and everyone laughs. Anna continues to note in her journal that Sarah is good for Papa. She helps him forget his worries and gets him to laugh again.

What we will cover in this chapter:

History and Geography: Church—How It Served the Community

Science: Cows—Herbivores

Career Paths: Astronaut and Astronomer

Lesson Activities:

History and Geography: Church—How It Served the Community

The Wittings enjoy going to church (page 14). Not only because it is their place of worship, but for other reasons as well. They are able to see friends and neighbors they don't see very often, visit and share stories.

Share with your student the place churches had in the past. For communities, particularly communities of pioneers spread far apart, after Sunday morning services was their only time for visiting. Families supported one another and were able to find out what the others needed. Without the aid of telephones or quick mail service, communicating with friends was difficult in those days. Therefore, churches became social gatherings for the congregation as well as a source of spiritual refreshment.

Encourage your student to look for old, small churches in and around the place where he lives. These old churches were generally just one or two rooms and often had a graveyard beside or behind them. Families generally attended the same church for generations, and as family members passed away they would be laid to rest in the site directly adjacent to their church.

What does your student think it would have been like to have lived during a time when he only got to see his friends once a week—on Sunday? How important would that gathering be?

Science: Cows—Herbivores

Mame and her new calf, Moonbeam, are certainly loved by the Wittings (page 17). Mame is a cow—cows are female cattle. The male cattle are called bulls. Has your student ever studied cattle? Fascinating from both a scientific and a sociological point of view, cattle are an important section of life science.

[**Teacher's Note**: For simplicity, this lesson will refer to the animal as a 'cow.' Do make note, however, for your student that this is the female term.]

Cows are gigantic animals—and there are more than 250 different breeds. Some of the most famous breeds are the Guernsey, Jerseys, Holstein, Angus and Herefords. Weighing between 1,000 and 3,000 pounds, they are impressive creatures. All cows grow horns, but many farmers cut the horns off the cattle when they are young. Cows are what are called 'herbivores.' They eat plants, not meat (meat-eating animals would be called carnivores). Cows generally eat grass, hay, clover and corn. They do not have any top teeth, but instead simply bite, chew a little and then swallow large mouthfuls of food. Cows also drink a lot of water—nearly 20 gallons a day! Can your student imagine drinking that much? (Humans are encouraged to consume eight 8-ounce glasses of water a day—how much more do cows drink?) Dairy cattle (cows used for milking) are usually milked twice a day by farmers. One cow can give almost 6 gallons of milk a day—nearly 100 glasses of milk!

Because cows are herbivores, their bodies are set up in a special way to digest all the roughage they consume. Instead of just one stomach, cows have four! Share with your student some information about this unusual digestive system.

When a cow chews its food for the first time, it isn't able to break the fibers down very much (no top teeth and the grass is tough!). After the cow swallows, the partially chewed food travels to the first stomach called the rumen. The rumen can hold nearly 50 gallons of food! In the rumen there are also vital enzymes and bacteria which help break down the food for the cow. Without these bacterium, the cow would not be able to digest any of its food.

The food is then regurgitated (or spit back up) in the cow's mouth and the cow again chews on it for awhile. This partially digested food is called the cud. Has your student ever heard of a "cow chewing her cud?"

When the cow has successfully chewed the food a second time, it is swallowed a second time and it now passes to a stomach called the reticulum. Then it passes to a third stomach called the omasum. Both of these stomachs provide nearly the same function—to rid the food of all its moisture—allowing the cow to fully absorb the water.

Finally, the food travels to the fourth stomach called the abomasum, where it meets acid and enzymes to fully digest the proteins. The abomasum is the only one of the four stomachs much like our own.

From there, the food (like the food we eat) goes through the small intestine and then large intestine.

If your student is interested, it might be helpful to make a drawing, somewhat like a flowchart, of the different digestive stages in a cow.

Besides providing the people of the world with milk and meat, cows are fascinating animals to study!

Career Paths: Astronaut and Astronomer

Papa likened the new calf's face to a "pale winter moon" (page 18). Has your student ever enjoyed just gazing at the moon? Has he ever wondered why a winter moon looks more pale than a summer moon? Is he interested in the stars or planets? Does he enjoy science and math? Perhaps a career in astronomy is just the thing he should begin to explore.

Astronomers study the stars, planets and space every day to learn more about our universe. They use massive telescopes (some as big as whole rooms) to see distant celestial sights. Astronomers also use a tool called a radio telescope. Instead of collecting visible light and displaying it to the human eye, a radio telescope collects invisible light in the form of energy. A radio telescope can be used during the day, as easily as at night and can tell the temperature in space! Spectrascopes are used by astronomers to determine the age, makeup and distance of stars.

But beyond telescopes, astronomers also use a variety of other tools, like cameras and computers. Some astronomers work in observatories, planetariums, or even as teachers in universities all over the world.

[Teacher's Note: If your student shows any interest in astronomy, a delightful and beneficial field trip would be to your area planetarium. Your student will learn a great deal and the instruction he receives from the tour guide will further deepen and solidify his understanding of this section. Many children have had life-long interests in astronomy sparked by an early trip to a planetarium.]

In order to become an astronomer, several years of concentrated study are required. Key subjects for students interested in astronomy are mathematics, physics, life and earth science.

[**Teacher's Note**: A fabulous resource for more information on career paths in astronomy as well as the other sciences is called *VGM's Career Portraits: Science*, by Jane Kelsey (Copyright 1997, ISBN 0844243779). This book includes great descriptions of each career, a question and answer section and then interviews with people in each career field.]

Here are some names your student might wish to use for research—all are famous American astronomers: Percival Lowell, Edwin Hubble, Williamina Fleming and Maria Mitchell. A book report, imaginary 'interview,' or poster board depicting the life of an astronomer—all would make wonderful assigned learning projects.

After discussing astronomy with your student, this would also make an excellent time to bring up perhaps the most famous "moon" career choice—an astronaut.

[**Teacher's Note**: Your student may have heard the term 'cosmonaut' before in reference to an astronaut. Cosmonaut is the word for astronaut in the former Soviet Union.]

The word 'astronaut' comes from the Greek words meaning 'sailor among the stars.'

Wanting to become an astronaut is a high goal. Astronauts are highly trained, specialized personnel who do a variety of jobs. Being able to control and fix a shuttle, understand the checklists and goals of the voyage, successfully maneuver in space in a bulky space suit, conduct scientific experiments regarding the planet Earth, monitor and program the high-tech science laboratory equipment on board, and of course, to have incredible bravery are just a few of the requirements for an astronaut.

When you are an astronaut, you work for a government agency called NASA (National Aeronautics and Space Administration).

Astronauts, called mission specialists, perform a variety of tasks. Some drop off equipment (like satellites), and others go to those equipment sites to repair them. Working nearly 16-hour workdays, mission specialists are in charge of performing the experiments, compiling observation logs (information on pollution, atmospheric conditions, weather patterns, etc.), maintaining the space craft, and even photo sessions of the planets and space.

Pilot astronauts are generally career officers in the Air Force or Navy and they command and control the flight of the aircraft.

NASA accepts applications to become an astronaut on a continuing basis. But, there are a few very specific requirements (one of which, is not age). First, the applicant must be a U.S. citizen and must have earned a bachelor's degree (or higher) in engineering, biological or physical science, or mathematics. All candidates must prove their physical and mental fitness during a week-long physical exam and interview.

Pilot astronaut candidates are required to have flown at least 1,000 in-command hours in a high-powered jet aircraft. They must also be between 64 and 76 inches in height. Mission specialist candidates don't need any flight experience, but they can only be between 60 and 76 inches tall. Why does your student think these height requirements are put in place?

If your student is interested in any aspect of astronomy or becoming an astronaut, encourage his interest by helping him write to a few of the following organizations for more information. Becoming an astronomer or astronaut requires bravery, a keen mind and an interest in the universe and learning all there is to know about it.

> NASA Headquarters
> 300 E. Street, S.W.
> Washington, DC 20546-0001

Write for more information and educational materials.

> Future Astronaut Training Program
> Kansas Cosmosphere & Space Center
> 1100 North Plum
> Hutchison, KS 67501

A five-day summer program for middle schoolers, designed to enhance interest in space science and related career development.

> Pacific Rim Spaceflight Academy
> Oregon Museum of Science and Industry
> 4015 S.W. Canyon Road
> Portland, OR 97221

Space camp programs available for ages eight through sixteen.

> The Young Astronaut Council
> P.O. Box 65432
> Washington, DC 20036

This is a private organization for elementary and junior high school students that creates materials and activities to stimulate interest in science, math and technology. Chapters may be formed in schools or neighborhoods.

Writing and Discussion Question

On page 15, Sarah says, "I'm surrounded by motherhood." Anna thinks her voice sounds "sad and thoughtful." Do you think Sarah would like to have a baby of her own? Give some reasons from the story (examples from both books are appropriate) to support your answer.

Vocabulary Words

rumen: the first stomach of an animal; food lands almost immediately after being swallowed

regurgitate: to spit back up after being swallowed

cud: the partially digested food the animal chews again

reticulum: second stomach of an animal which continues the digestive process

omasum: third stomach, continues to digest the food

abomasum: a fourth stomach where the food meets acids and enzymes to fully digest the proteins

Internet Connections

To view current suggested links relating to this chapter's lessons, see www.fiveinarow.com/connections.

Chapter 4

Parent Summary

One day Papa comes home from town with letters for Sarah from her three aunts in Maine—Harriet, Mattie and Lou. Sarah sits and reads from the letters to the whole family by lamp light that night. Unlike the Wittings' experience on the prairie with the drought, Maine is getting a lot of rain. "Two inches by the glass measure...," Aunt Mattie's letter says. Caleb immediately asks what a "glass measure" is, but no one explains. Everyone is thinking about the rain and how much it is needed on the prairie. Sarah feels bad about reading the letters to Papa. She doesn't want him to feel worse about the drought.

That night, Caleb sets a small glass on a fence post out in the yard. He tells Sarah he did it for Papa—the glass is waiting for rain.

What we will cover in this chapter:

History and Geography: Droughts and Floods—Your State's History

Science: Building Your Own Weather Station

Issues of Human Relationships: Optimism and Hope

Lesson Activities

History and Geography: Droughts and Floods—Your State's History

The Wittings' home and the surrounding land is experiencing a terrible drought. Where does your student live? Chances are, even if not in his lifetime, wherever he lives your student's state has had periods of flooding and of drought. Why not do some research and find out when those times were?

At your local library, your student can obtain books (generally in the reference section) referring to the regional weather. Called 'almanacs,' these books contain hundreds of tables of information graphing and calculating the high temperatures, low temperatures and average rainfall (or lack of) for your student's area. By asking a librarian for assistance, these books can be easily located and can provide wonder information.

After he has compiled a few interesting facts about his area (perhaps the longest period of time without rain, the most rainfall in a given 24-hour period, etc.), your student can create a poster or drawing to depict his findings. By drawing an outline of his city or state, he can pinpoint and identify specific regions or areas where floods or droughts have occurred. He can even create a timeline at the bottom or around the sides of the poster, giving comparisons of weather events with other major events. Find library books on weather, droughts and floods to supplement your student's research.

Science: Building Your Own Weather Station

Caleb is very interested in this 'glass for rain' concept (page 23). Does your student understand how this works? In very simple terms, a glass set out for a period of time will collect the rainfall and then each morning, you can measure how much has fallen—

one inch, two inches, etc. Your student can create a rain measuring device (called a rain gauge) as easily as Caleb did, by simply setting a glass outside on a tabletop or deck. However, why not take this idea a step further?

Quite easily, using everyday materials, your student can create his own "weather station." He can build instruments that will measure temperature, air pressure, rainfall, wind direction and speed, and humidity.

First, have your student create a record-keeping chart. There should be a column for the date and then subsequent columns with the categories he wishes to track: temperature, dew point, clouds, wind, rain, etc. Using this chart each day or week, will allow your student to compare his findings to the meteorologists on television/radio, and can assist him in making predictions of his own.

The first piece of equipment your student will probably want to include in his weather station is a thermometer. Although these can be made at home, it is much easier (and will provide more accuracy) to simply buy an inexpensive indoor/outdoor thermometer at any hardware or discount shop. You can usually find these thermometers for under $10.

Next, a rain gauge can be created by using a clear plastic bowl or glass, some masking tape and a waterproof marker. Have your student place a vertical strip of masking tape on the side of the container. Then, with a waterproof marker, he can mark off a measuring scale by the inch, quarter-inch or eighths. Remind your student, if he is comparing his records to that of the weatherman's and finds they differ, that rainfall can differ greatly from one area to the next—even from one side of a street to the next! What the weatherman generally reports is the average rainfall—the entire area's measurements averaged to one figure.

Your student can create his own barometer to measure air pressure. This is what he will need: a saucer or bowl, water, masking tape, a pen and an empty, clean, plastic soda bottle.

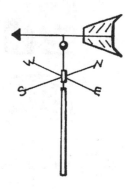

First, help your student fill the saucer halfway with water. Fill the bottle with water until it is almost full. With your help and supervision (and maybe outdoors), your student should put his thumb over the mouth of the bottle and invert it onto the saucer. When it is in place, upside down, have him remove his thumb quickly and steady the bottle. (Strips of tape from the bottom of the bottle to the sides of the saucer can help secure it.) Now, have your student place a strip of masking tape to the side of the bottle and have him mark the water level and the date.

Why doesn't the water in the bottle pour out? The air pressure inside the bottle is pressing down and prevents the water from running out. When the air pressure changes, so will the water level. An increase in air pressure sends the water level inside the bottle up. A decrease in air pressure allows it to drop down. When the water in the bottle drops down (low air pressure), you can usually predict warmer, wetter weather. When the water is high (high pressure), you can usually predict less humid, dryer weather.

The dew point is the temperature at which the surrounding air can no longer hold all the water vapor it contains. Then, some of that vapor begins to change back to liquid form (condensation) and form droplets. The closer the dew point temperature is to the air temperature, the more likely it is that you will have rain or snow.

[**Teacher's Note**: You will find a complete lesson on dew point and frost in *Beyond Five in a Row,* Volume 1, in the *Thomas Edison* unit, chapter 3 lesson activities.]

Here are the things your student will need to create his dew point thermometer: a metal soup can (washed and de-labeled), water, ice cubes and a thermometer.

First, have your student record the current temperature. Next, fill the can with water and then make sure the outside of the can is very dry. Place the thermometer in the water and begin adding ice cubes, one at a time. Carefully stir it with the thermometer. Watch both the sides of the can and the thermometer. As the temperature goes down, liquid beads begin to form on the outside of the can. The temperature the thermometer reads, at the point at which liquid begins to form on the can is at, or near, the 'dew point.'

There are more science weather measuring devices your student can build and add to his weather station, but these are enough to get him started. Encourage him to record each day, or week, his findings and to compare those to the professionals. Encourage him to make his own predictions and to do further research on his own (if there is interest) on weather, at the library or his local bookstore.

You might even wish to call your local television station and see if you can arrange a tour and a visit with the meteorologist. Just like Caleb, your student can measure the rainfall—just hope there is more to measure than at the Wittings' house.

Issues of Human Relationships: Optimism and Hope

Caleb demonstrates his optimism by placing his rain glass on the fence post (page 23). Had there been any rain in their area recently? Was there any prospect? No. But, Caleb isn't going to be discouraged. He has hope.

Each of us has a choice. We can choose to embrace hope and faith, believing the best in every situation, or we can choose not to believe, expecting nothing positive in life. The choice we make will impact our own life and the lives of those around us. Encourage your student to cultivate an attitude of optimism, embracing hope and faith in his daily life. By believing the best about others, and by not allowing ourselves to develop a negative attitude, we can encourage those around us and make the most of our own life.

Writing and Discussion Question

On page 22, we read, "There was more that Sarah hadn't read..." Why didn't Sarah read all of the letters to Jacob? What was her motive in concealing parts of the letter? Why does Anna cry when she reads the part in the letters that Sarah skipped?

Internet Connections

To view current suggested links relating to this chapter's lessons, see www.fiveinarow.com/connections.

Chapter 5

Parent Summary

The water level in the Wittings' well drops lower and lower, and Papa decides they will have to go to town to haul water for the animals. When they get there, Sarah runs into Maggie who is comforting another friend, Caroline. Caroline and her husband Joseph are being forced to move because of the drought. Their well is completely dry. Sarah is forced to see the painful, very real result of a drought. She is frustrated and overcome with sadness.

What we will cover in this chapter:

History and Geography: Food and Water—People Follow

Science: Moving in the Heat—Heat Exhaustion

Fine Arts: The Colors of Drought—No Green

Lesson Activities

History and Geography: Food and Water—People Follow

On page 27, we see Caroline and Joseph being forced to move. Their well has gone dry, and they have no choice. People, just like animals, must have water to survive. During times of drought (as in times of famine), people tend to follow food and water.

[**Teacher's Note**: If you did the unit study on *The Boxcar Children* from *Beyond Five in a Row,* Volume 1 (page 44), you may have shared the lesson on the 'Irish Potato Famine' with your student. Here is an excerpt from that lesson: Because of the lack of industry, the Irish relied mainly on agriculture for both their livelihood and their food. Potatoes became the main staple for most of the impoverished Irish people. A plant disease attacked the potato plants in 1845, and for the next three years people began dying from lack of food. Approximately one million people lost their lives due to what is now known as the 'Great Potato Famine.' Further study on this tragic time in Ireland's history could serve as an excellent research or speech project for your student, as you discuss the concept of famine and drought.]

In the United States, we have a great diversity of land types—prairies, mountains, bays and deserts. The desert regions, chiefly located in the Southwest (Arizona, New Mexico, Utah, Nevada and areas of California), were virtually uninhabited by people as recently as 150 years ago. Except for the Native Americans and Mexican-Americans who were already accustomed to living without much water, and who had learned to adapt their crops and food sources to the surrounding desert, people were not able to migrate to those regions. Today, however, millions of Americans call these areas of desert their home, thanks to land reclamation.

Land reclamation is the word used to describe converting unusable land to farmland and usable housing, commercial or industrial areas. Land reclamation involves various ways to irrigate crop fields and to build and make use of various aqueducts and water sources foreign to the region naturally. Desert soil can become quite rich and fertile soil for farming (or for growing a lawn), because there is no rain to wash away chemicals the plants need. Mechanically controlled sprinklers are the most common way to irrigate farm fields. Water trickle hoses are used on many lawns and golf courses.

[**Teacher's Note**: Sometimes wet, marshy land is also reclaimed by draining it of excess water, building retaining walls or filling and raising it to be dry and useful.]

Certain regions of land in the world are in constant water shortage, because they never get enough rain. However, drought can even strike areas that normally have average rainfall, and can do so quite suddenly. In the 1960s, regions of the Northeastern United States, as well as parts of China, Brazil and Portugal were stricken with drought, while simultaneously, flood waters drenched and damaged massive areas in the Midwestern United States and in Mexico.

Learning about water conservation, land reclamation and caring for our environment are all ways even young people can take part in managing our land and water supplies.

Science: Moving in the Heat—Heat Exhaustion

Read with your student the following sentence on page 26—"*Everything seemed to move slow in town, as if the heat had taken over.*" Take this time to discuss with your student heat exhaustion and other ways heat affects the human body.

Has your student ever noticed when the weather is very hot he often doesn't feel like running or playing? Why is that? The human body has an internal thermometer. Our temperature, when it is normal, should read 98.6° F. As in many areas, our bodies somewhat self-monitor themselves. Your body knows when it is losing heat, as well as gaining heat. When we are outdoors and the sun is beating down, we may feel a bit sluggish or slow moving. Our brains are telling us we shouldn't be moving too quickly, or we could overheat. If we ignore our body's warning and exert a great deal of energy, we can overheat. When this happens it is called heat exhaustion or heatstroke. Either of these conditions can be quite serious.

Your body helps itself maintain the right temperature through several means, one of which is sweating. Did you have any idea sweating was a positive, healthy thing? When you sweat, the beads of water form all over your body, and as they evaporate, your skin cools slightly. That drop in temperature, caused by evaporation, helps keep you cool and your internal thermometer happy. But what happens if you get too hot, too quickly?

Heatstroke sometimes affects people when they have been working in excessive heat for a very long time. Scientists have found, the longer you are in hot temperatures, the less you sweat. And remember, the less you sweat, the hotter you are going to become. Unfortunately, people often don't even notice when they quit sweating. If left unchecked, a heatstroke victim's temperature can easily exceed 110° F., and require immediate hospitalization. Heatstroke victims can also experience pulse weakening, irregular breathing, and lightheadedness, as well as the lack of perspiration. First aid recommendations for heatstroke are fairly simple. The most important thing is to quickly lower the person's temperature. This can be done by submerging him in a cool bathtub of water and/or applying cold compresses to his forehead, pulse points and the back of his neck.

A slightly less serious heat condition, and even more common, is called heat exhaustion. Heat exhaustion occurs when people work or play in areas of high heat and high humidity. Although the person may continue to sweat freely, his body temperature may begin falling below normal (unlike heatstroke where the temperature escalates). A heat exhaustion patient may become weak and dizzy, and may even vomit. Someone experiencing heat exhaustion must be taken to a cooler area. People who suffer from heat exhaustion frequently take salt tablets to compensate for the salt loss in their sweat.

It is both interesting and important that your student understand the ways heat affects our bodies—and how to help someone in need.

Fine Arts: The Colors of Drought—No Green

On page 26, MacLachlan offers us an unusual description of the prairie. Because of the drought, the land has become dry and dusty. We read, "...as far as I could see the fields were brown...There was no green." What does your student think that would look like? Land stretched out as far as you could see without a blade or spot of green?

Taking MacLachlan's description, encourage your student to paint or draw a picture reflecting the words—"There was no green." Perhaps he would use only shades of blue for the sky, and shades of sienna, brown and tan for the earth and trees. Or he could sketch a picture of the prairie, drawn completely in shades of brown. Allow your student's imagination to run wild and see what he can create!

Writing and Discussion Question

On the first line of chapter 5 we read, "Each day Papa dropped a rope with a stone down the well to measure the water level." By writing an informative or technical paragraph, describe how this would work—think through the process. How did Papa use a rope and stone to measure the water level? You may even wish to draw a diagram to accompany your explanation.

Vocabulary Words

land reclamation: converting deserts to farmland and usable housing areas, through irrigation options

heatstroke: collapse or sudden illness with fever and dry skin, caused by overexposure to excessive heat

heat exhaustion: a condition caused by excessive exposure to heat and characterized by cold, clammy hands and general symptoms of shock

Internet Connections

To view current suggested links relating to this chapter's lessons, see www.fiveinarow.com/connections.

Chapter 6

Parent Summary

On their way home from town, the Wittings see a fire in their meadow. Quickly, they work together to soak down sacks and beat the fire back. The fire is soon out, but Papa warns the family they must be on constant alert for fire from now on—the drought is causing everything to be dry and a fire hazard.

What we will cover in this chapter:

[**Teacher's Note**: This particular chapter was rich with lesson ideas surrounding the topic of fire. It might be interesting for your student to complete the following lessons and keep his notes and research in a separate folder or journal, thus compiling a complete unit study on fire and related topics.]

History and Geography: Fires in History—The Great Chicago Fire

History and Geography: Geographic Areas Where Fire Is a Constant Risk

Science: Fire—The Chemical and Scientific Background

Language Arts: Learning to Interview

Fine Arts: How to Create your Own 'Fire'—Tips from the Stage

Fine Arts: A Famous 'Fire' Poem by William Blake: "The Tyger"

Issues of Human Relationships: Health and Safety—Fire Precautions

Issues of Human Relationships: Health and Safety—First Aid

Issues of Human Relationships: Being a Person of Commitment

Career Path: Firefighter

Lesson Activities

History and Geography: Fires in History—The Great Chicago Fire

The Wittings' fire was relatively easy to stop. With hard work and wet sacks, the family is able to beat it back and control the flames (page 33). Sometimes, however, fires cannot be put out so easily. Throughout history, famous fires have occurred which changed people's lives and destroyed entire cities. One of the most famous fires in the United States was the Great Chicago Fire of October 8, 1871. Share with your student the story and the surrounding myths of this famous disaster.

In the late 19th century, most buildings were built of wood. Those that were not (constructed mostly of brick or stone), certainly weren't equipped with modern-day fire protection, i.e., fire walls, fire retardant curtains, fire extinguishers, etc.

Most of Chicago, a booming metropolis of that day, was constructed of wood (a few building were made of brick, iron or stone). The population at that time had soared to nearly 350,000 people and was rapidly growing. Just like the Wittings experienced, during that summer of 1871 Chicago had suffered a great drought. According to legend, late on the night of October 7, a Mrs. O'Leary was milking her cow out in her barn. Mrs. O'Leary made her living selling milk to her working class, Irish neighborhood. Supposedly, that evening her cow got riled and kicked over Mrs. O'Leary's lantern. The straw and barn caught fire almost immediately and with the dry grasses and the strong winds, the fire spread rapidly north and northeast. Nearly 30 buildings were consumed before the fire department could even arrive at the scene.

Throughout the night, 90 firefighters (nearly half of the city's department) worked tirelessly to fight the flames. The fire reached the waterworks of the city sometime around midnight, and the pumps were ruined. There was now no way to fight the fire. Miraculously, rain began to fall around the same time and by 3:00 a.m. on October 8, the fire was finally out. The new day revealed more than 20 acres of Chicago's West Side burned to the ground. Thirty firefighters died, 300 people lost their lives and one-third of the city was utterly destroyed. More than 18,000 homes were destroyed, leaving tens of thousands homeless. The city was virtually wiped out.

The story of Mrs. O'Leary and her cow has become more than a legend as the years have passed. Although many believe that is actually the way the fire started, other critics and lawyers have continued to search for more answers even as recently at 1997. Another culprit recently cited is a Mr. Daniel Sullivan, a one-legged horse-cart driver who was a neighbor of Mrs. O'Leary's—and who may have, in fact, been in her barn lighting a lantern or smoking a pipe on that night, October 7. Whether or not it's true will probably never be known. In any event, the story of Mrs. O'Leary has become an historic legend, a part of Chicago's mythology. It has been said, "This is the city a cow kicked over." Songs have been written about the event. The first verse to one of these goes like this:

Late last night, when we were all in bed
Old Lady Leary left a lantern in the shed
When the cow kicked it over, she winked her eye and said,
"There'll be a hot time in the old town tonight."

A movie about the fire, entitled *In Old Chicago,* came out in 1938 starring Don Ameche and Alice Brady (who incidentally, won a Oscar for the role).

If there is interest, encourage your student to do more of his own research into this famous American disaster. Perhaps he can uncover clues regarding the real story of the Great Chicago Fire. There have also been many other famous city fires. Here are a few more for research and report possibilities: San Francisco, CA—1906; New York City, NY—1911; Boston, MA—1942; and Mexico City, Mexico—1988.

The Wittings were certainly lucky they were able to control their fire, weren't they?

History and Geography:
Geographic Areas Where Fire Is a Constant Risk

Fires can be dangerous and risky, no matter where you live. However, there are certain areas of the United States where fires are much more of a problem. Certainly, where the Wittings live on the prairie, it is a risk. With low rainfall and fields of hay and crops, fire can spread quickly (page 32).

Generally, in the United States the highest risk areas are in California and the Northwestern prairies (Idaho, Wyoming and Montana). Each year, fires rage through various areas in these regions, often consuming many acres.

Interesting to note for your student, not only do fires consume people's homes and businesses and destroy forests and parks, they also cost a great deal of money. The monetary losses from fires can be astounding. In 1991, the Oakland Hills, CA, fire resulted in a $1.5 billion loss. In 1992, in Los Angeles, CA, riots and fires resulted in $567 million in property damages. And in Idaho, it is state law to bill all people responsible for forest fires. In a recent decision, Fred and Jeanne Howard have been billed over $1 million dollars for a fire they started in July, 1992.

Where does your student live? Has he ever seen or been near a large forest fire or prairie fire? What was it like? If your student lives in a high-risk fire area, he is probably already aware of the dangers and the precautions your area takes. If not, why not take some time to research and study a specific region of the country and the fires which have occurred there.

Science: Fire—The Chemical and Scientific Background

[**Teacher's Note**: Before doing this lesson, it might be beneficial and fun to light a candle and observe the flame with your student. See what questions he has—or how much he already knows.]

As we have seen in this chapter, fire can be a dangerous and destructive thing. But what exactly is it? Does your student know the chemical make-up of fire? What makes the flame look blue at the base, then red, then orange and sometimes yellow at the top? What makes it hot?

Fire is the word used to describe the combination of heat and light that come from burning substances. A famous French chemist, Antoine Lavoisier, proved in 1777 that burning (and thereby sometimes fire) is the chemical result of oxygen combining with other substances. When, for example, iron is combined with oxygen (which is present in the air), a slow change develops called rust. This is known as oxidation. When the same process occurs more quickly, for example, oxygen combining with gasoline, the action causes heat to be given off quickly. The process is called combustion.

For fire to occur, three things must be present. First, a fuel or substance that will burn is necessary (solids: examples are wood or coal; liquids: oil or gasoline; and gases: natural gas or hydrogen). There must also be heat—enough heat to raise the temperature of the air (and oxygen) to a combustible point. This temperature is called the kindling temperature. Finally, there must be oxygen present—usually from the air.

For a fire to start, it is often necessary for the proportions of flame to substance to be fairly equal. For example, it might be difficult for your student to get a giant log burning from a single match. On the other hand, a small stick or twig might burn quite easily. This is because there is more oxygen surrounding the twig in relation to the burning match than there is around the large log. Sometimes, when people build campfires, you'll notice them fanning the flames. Why? Because the slight wind brings more air (and thereby more oxygen) into contact with the beginning flame. The fire is, therefore, more likely to continue burning brightly.

[**Teacher's Note**: If you covered the unit on *Thomas Edison* in *Beyond Five in a Row*, Volume 1, you may have done the lesson on the chemical element phosphorus, located in chapter 13 of that unit. Phosphorus must be kept wet (even submerged in water). It is extremely flammable. Its kindling temperature is so low, it can become combustible in normal air temperatures. If you already did this lesson, you may wish to take this time to go back and review it with your student.]

Ask your student whether or not he thinks fire can totally consume a piece of wood. Is there anything left? Actually, although the flames will destroy most of it, fire cannot entirely burn a piece of wood. What about the ashes? What are they? When you see ashes and bits of charred black pieces left in the bottom of a fireplace or fire pit, what you are seeing are the remains of a log. Ashes are a mixture of minerals present in the wood that are inflammable. Different fuels produce different amounts of ash—this ratio is known as the ash content.

[**Teacher's Note**: If your student shows interest in this topic, other fascinating related subjects for study are: matches, spontaneous combustion and smoke.]

Language Arts: Learning to Interview

Imagine how frightened and tired Papa and Sarah were after they beat out the fire! What a story they would have to tell. Does your student know anyone who has been in some kind of natural disaster such as a fire, flood, tornado, earthquake, etc.? If he knows someone who is willing to share his or her story, take this opportunity to help your student develop interviewing skills, as well as work on writing techniques.

Interviewing someone for a writing project can be a fascinating and rewarding venture. It might seem simple to some students, but there are several key guidelines you should always follow.

First, call or contact the person you're interested in interviewing and share with them your ideas for the project. If the person is willing to participate, it is appropriate to set up an interview time. It is also wise to share with the interviewee a few of the questions you will be asking. In this way, he can be prepared for you.

Next, it is important to do your own research on the topics beforehand. This will help give you background on the situation and will help you formulate intelligent questions. For example, if you are interviewing someone who was in an earthquake, it would be advantageous to look up some information on earthquakes and possibly some other people's stories concerning their experiences.

When you are at the interview itself, it is always a good idea to take a pencil, notepad and a tape recorder, if possible. Your questions should already be written out, but never limit yourself to only these ideas. If something arises in conversation and you have a new question, go with your instinct. Sometimes the best ideas, quotes and stories come from within the interview itself. The tape recorder will help you get accurate quotes when you are writing the article, but it is important to make brief hand-written notes throughout the interview. If something happens to the tape, you will still have responses recorded.

When you are ready to write your article, using the quotes and story from the interview, remember—it is vital you quote accurately. If you have any doubts about something that was said—a date or time, a person's name, etc.—always double check! Now you're ready to write!

Fine Arts: How to Create Your Own 'Fire'—Tips from the Stage

The flames and heat the Wittings fought in their field were not fake, but quite real. However sometimes, in old movies and on the stage, technicians create 'fake' fire. Has your student ever been interested in special effects or technical theatre work? Here is a simple project your student can create which will teach him a little about both.

To create your own 'fire' you will need: sticks and twigs, a small fan, a flashlight, scissors and cellophane paper (yellow, red or orange are preferred).

First, have your student cut flame-shaped strips from the cellophane paper. He can cut as many as he thinks are needed, in whatever shape he thinks looks realistic. If he has a choice in colors, he may wish to experiment with several different combinations of red, orange, yellow or even blue.

Next, have your student (in a room which can be made fairly dark) arrange the twigs and sticks in whatever pattern he wants for his 'fire'—perhaps in a circle like a campfire or a pyramid shape like a bonfire. When he has the wood arranged, he should take his fire strips and in some way attach them to the underneath section of the twigs. Hot glue (used with supervision), 'super' glue, or strong duct tape all work fairly well. The logs can be taped together, too, so they will stay in their pattern. However, enough of the cellophane strips should be left free in the middle of the wood (where the flames would be in an actual fire).

Now, he needs to set up a practice session. By placing a flashlight against or under the wood and turning it on, your student should be able to achieve a glowing effect. By positioning a small fan behind the logs and the strips of paper, he can make the flames 'come alive' and flicker, like real flames.

Finally, with the lights turned off and everything set, your student can sit back and marvel at his special effects. Imagine! With paper, light and wind he has created fire! For even more effect, if there is interest, your student can tape record fire sounds from a real campfire or fireplace blaze and then play them during his demonstration. Have fun! This type of exercise is an avenue for creativity. It also builds 'problem solving' skills as your student tries to see what will work best. This exercise will also help your student become more observant as he looks to see how media and entertainment special effects are created.

Fine Arts: A Famous 'Fire' Poem by William Blake: "The Tyger"

Fire is a fascinating topic and image. A poet named William Blake wrote a now famous poem using flame as a main image. Share with your student some information about this poet and the poem.

William Blake (1757-1827) was a painter and poet. All of his artistic endeavors showed a great sense of imagination and creativity. His colors, his word choices, and his philosophies were unconventional and astounding. Blake was born in London, England and lived most of his life there. He was, by profession, an illustrator and engraver.

Perhaps one of his most beautiful poems is entitled "The Tyger." Share this amazing poem with your student. It is well suited for memorization and recitation. If your student is willing and interested, assign the poem and then have him recite it for a parent or grandparent. This sharpens memorization and public speaking skills. Perhaps your

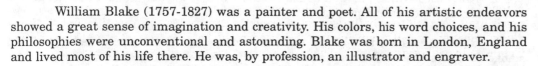

student would like to draw or paint a picture to correspond with the poem. You may use it as a practice piece for your student's penmanship practice.

The Tyger

Tyger! Tyger! burning bright
In the forests of the night,
What immortal hand or eye
Could frame thy fearful symmetry?

In what distant deeps or skies
Burnt the fire of thine eyes?
On what wings dare he aspire?
What the hand dare seize the fire?

And what shoulder, and what art,
Could twist the sinews of thy heart?
And when thy heart began to beat,
What dread hand? And what dread feet?

What the hammer? What the chain?
In what furnace was thy brain?
What the anvil? What the grasp
Dare its deadly terrors clasp?

When the stars threw down their spears,
And watered heaven with their tears,
Did he smile his work to see?
Did he who made the Lamb make thee?

Tyger! Tyger! burning bright
In the forests of the night,
What immortal hand or eye
Dare frame thy fearful symmetry?

What does your student think Blake is trying to understand by writing this poem? Is it just about a tiger? Enjoy this poem with your student today, and allow the metaphors and images to ignite more discussion.

Issues of Human Relationships: Health and Safety—Fire Precautions

Sometimes fires just start—like the Wittings' fire in their field. The grass is dry and accidents happen. But is it possible to take precautions and prevent fires? Yes! Ask your student if he has ever heard of a fire escape map or the words: stop, drop and roll? Does he know how to operate a fire extinguisher and remember where it is located in his house?

All of these things, as well as many others are ways your student and his family can protect themselves and prevent many dangerous fires.

Remind your student of the main protections he should always have in place: smoke detectors on each floor of his house (perhaps several detectors, depending upon the layout), fire extinguishers in at least the kitchen, basement and garage, and a fire escape map charted and practiced for his family.

A fire escape *map* is basically a plan of action, in case of emergency. Each family member should have a clear understanding of what doors or windows from which they can exit and how to do so quickly! Always remember: if there is a fire in your home, DO NOT STOP for pets or pictures or anything else, just GET OUT! That is the *number one* rule for safety. The second rule is once out, never go back in for anything and hold all little children so they do not run back into a burning building. Once a fire escape map has been charted and discussed, it is always good to practice a few times. If there were a real fire, the smoke and heat (and your known nerves) would be confusing enough. It would be better if the escape route had been rehearsed in advance.

Here is a list of other Do's and Don'ts:

Don't leave electrical appliances (coffee makers, irons, hot plates, etc.) on and unattended.

Don't overload your electrical circuits.

Don't leave bare or splintered wires and cords out. Wrap them or dispose of them.

Don't leave candles or other open flames unattended.

Don't try to move or carry a contained fire.

Don't use an elevator to escape a fire.

Don't open a door that is hot to the touch.

Don't re-enter a burning building for any reason.

Do clean and maintain your fireplaces and chimneys.

Do properly dispose of burnable trash.

Do teach fire safety to your friends and family.

Do teach the dangers of fireworks.

Do close your doors at night for added protection.

Do store and use any flammable liquids safely.

Remind your student of perhaps the most important tip of all: If he ever finds himself in the situation where his hair or clothes have caught on fire, STOP, DROP and ROLL! This will smother the flames and could save his life.

Learning about fire safety is just one more way we can protect ourselves and our loved ones, and help those in need!

Issues of Human Relationships: Health and Safety—First Aid

If your student has ever had a burn (even a small one) he knows how painful they can be. Some people argue a burn is much worse than a laceration, because of the slow healing process.

To treat a burn properly, care should be taken to cool the area immediately. By using water or cold compresses, the pain should subside somewhat. Never put butter or oil on a burn—that is an old wives' tale. Next, loosely bandage the burn with some gauze. The tighter the weave, the less likely it is the gauze will stick to the burn. Of course, for more serious third degree burns, professional help should be sought immediately.

If you have any questions about helping someone or treating yourself in a genuine emergency situation, always call 911 and seek more assistance.

If your student is interested in learning more about first aid and related topics, you might contact your local Red Cross or doctor and see what materials they have to offer. Also, getting trained in CPR is a wonderful activity for young people. It is interesting and provides them with a valuable skill!

Issues of Human Relationships: Being a Person of Commitment

Draw your student's attention to page 30 and the conversation between Papa and Sarah.

"Travel? Where would I go, Jacob?"
"Somewhere green," said Papa. "Somewhere cool."
Sarah looked at Papa.
"Do you think I would leave?" asked Sarah softly.
Papa was silent.

We see this same conversation arise a few pages later, when Sarah reiterates the question (page 34). What does your student think about this exchange? What do we know about Sarah thus far in our story? Is she a person of commitment? From what we have come to learn about Sarah, one could easily argue that she is, in fact, such a person. She left her only home and friends to come to the prairie in the first place. She obviously loves Jacob and the children very much. She has helped out during the squall, helped fix a roof, and she has also brought a lot of good times and memories to the Wittings. Sarah is a person of commitment. She's not likely to leave because things get difficult.

Learning to be a person of commitment is an important character journey. It doesn't take much to tell someone you'll help them out, but following through is different—particularly if you're extra tired or the day is filled with other activities. Keeping your word and staying with situations even when they are difficult is part of being mature and strong.

Encourage your student today by sharing with him a time when perhaps you were struggling to keep a commitment. How did you deal with that struggle? What have you learned about promises and character that you could share?

Being committed to people and tasks is a positive and productive way to live!

Career Path: Firefighter

Papa, Sarah and the children were forced to fight their fire alone, weren't they? They were able to beat it out. But what if it had been a larger fire? Anna would not be able to simply call 911 and ask for a fire truck, as we can today. How lucky we are to have firefighters who are willing to serve and protect us.

If your student is interested in helping people, enjoys being a part of emergency situations, and likes working on a team, then explore the career of a professional firefighter.

Firefighters are men and women who are expertly trained to assist and save lives in emergency situations. Firefighters never know what each workday will bring. A burning home with four people to help, a car accident, a kitchen fire, a warehouse fire, a heart attack victim—each could happen at any moment. When a firefighter goes to work, his or her shift lasts 24 hours! They must be prepared to handle all emergency calls any time during the day or night.

When firefighters are on duty, they live together and work together for the entire shift. Generally, the same team of fighters is on call together. Teamwork and sharing responsibilities is vital to make the station run smoothly.

It takes a good deal of courage to be a firefighter. These men and women risk their health and lives every day to help others. It takes a consistently positive attitude, creative problem solving skills, physical strength and endurance, and emotional maturity (to handle intense emergency situations). It also requires a good deal of compassion for people.

To become a firefighter, you can either take a twelve-week firefighter training program or study in a two-year program for an associate's degree in fire science, after graduating from high school.

If your student is interested in researching this career path further, there are several things you can do to help. First, call and arrange a tour of a fire station in your area. This will give him more insight into the job, as well as increase his knowledge of fire safety. The Boy Scouts of America has a tremendous resource called the Explorer Program. Through this organization, local fire departments work with teenagers, providing them with uniforms and instruction into the basics of fire fighting. Once a week the teens meet with professional firefighters. They receive general training in first aid, fire trucks and all the equipment. When they have been tested and are approved, the students can ride on the fire trucks. They are issued their own fire gear and can accompany the  firefighters on emergency calls. Although they are not allowed inside a burning building, this program is excellent for helping students discover the ins and outs of being a firefighter!

Students can begin the program as young as 14 and stay in until they are 20. Often these students, called cadets, are hired right out of the program as full-time firefighters.

For more information on this program, write:

Boy Scouts of America
Explorers Program
P.O. Box 152079
Irving, TX 75015

For more information on other careers in the firefighting field write:

International Association of Firefighters
1750 New York Avenue, N.W.
Washington, DC 20006

If your student is extremely interested and motivated to explore this career path further, he can obtain and browse through a sample fire fighting exam at his local library, by requesting:

Arco Firefighter by Robert Andriuolo, Deputy Chief, New York, Prentice Hall

This sample exam will give your student an idea of the questions and requirements a firefighting program will ask and demand.

Firefighters are brave and compassionate servants. Explore this challenging career path today!

Writing and Discussion Question

In our chapter, when Sarah asks Papa, "Do you really think I would leave?" Papa remains silent. If he had responded right away, what do you think he would have said? Does Jacob believe she might leave, or is he just frightened and stressed? What do you think Sarah will do?

Vocabulary Words

oxidation: the chemical result of oxygen combined with other substances

combustion: a rapid oxidation accompanied by heat and light

kindling temperature: the temperature of the air required to create combustion

Internet Connections

To view current suggested links relating to this chapter's lessons, see www.fiveinarow.com/connections.

Chapter 7

Parent Summary

Every day the drought worsens. The children aren't taking baths anymore to conserve water and each day requires the family to haul water for the animals. One day, as the Wittings near the river's edge they see Matthew and Maggie's wagon already parked there. Maggie is very sad. Soon the truth comes out. Matthew, Maggie, Rose and Violet are being forced to move because of the drought. They have no choice. Sarah is angry and doesn't understand why anyone would choose to live on the prairie. She tells Maggie (and Anna overhears) she hates the prairie—that she hates the land. Maggie tells her in order to survive here, you must love the land. She tells Sarah that Jacob was right. You have to write your name in the land to live here.

What we will cover in this chapter:

History and Geography:
Hauling Water—How Much Work It Really Takes

Language Arts: Analogies—A Comparison Easier to Understand

Language Arts: Imagery—Sarah's Voice

Fine Arts: Cooking—Biscuits

Lesson Activities

History and Geography:
Hauling Water—How Much Work It Really Takes

Papa, Sarah and the children must go every day to haul water in wooden barrels for the animals and themselves (page 38). How difficult a task is that? How much water do you think the Wittings had to haul?

Remind your student of the lesson on cattle located in the chapter 3 lessons of *Skylark*. In that reading, we learn that cattle drink nearly 20 gallons of water daily! That is just enough water for one cow or bull, and the Wittings have Mame, her calf and maybe a couple of others—not to mention the horses, the three chickens, Nick, Lottie and Seal. And those are just the animals we know of! In other words, they must have needed to haul a great deal of water.

But how difficult is it to haul water? Bring realism to this lesson by allowing your student to try his own hand at hauling water.

[**Teacher's Note**: This part of the lesson would probably be done best outside, in case an accident would occur.]

Let your student select a "barrel" of sorts to fill with water. (10-20 gallon plastic trash buckets work the best.) It must be large enough to hold a significant amount of water. Now, have your student fill it nearly full. Can he lift it? How many gallons does he have in the bucket? How many must he take out in order to carry it? Then work some calculations with him. If he can carry five gallons, and one cow drinks twenty in a day, that one animal will require four trips. Multiply that times 4 and you have sixteen back-breaking loads for only the cattle!

The story tells us the Wittings have ceased taking baths in order to save water, but what about washing dishes? Drinking water? Scrubbing their clothes? Cooking? When you stop and think about it, the amount of water a family needs from day to day is astounding.

Learning to conserve water and take care of our resources is one way we can help prevent water shortages and help our environment. Aren't you thankful you don't have to haul water like Papa and Sarah? Remind your student to be thankful the next time he takes a bath or shower!

Language Arts: Analogies—A Comparison Easier to Understand

Sarah is angry and sad her neighbors have to move away. Maggie tries to explain, but doesn't get far (page 40). Then she tells Sarah she reminds her of a prairie lark—"You are like a prairie lark, you know. It sings its song above the land to let all the birds know it's there before it plunges down to earth to make its home. But you have not come to earth, Sarah."

Why does Maggie offer this kind of explanation to Sarah? Why does she use a story of a bird? Sometimes when people are trying to explain a difficult concept or feeling they use what is known as an analogy. An analogy is a comparison of two things—often one complex example and one simpler example. Analogies help provide clarity. Maggie knew Sarah loves wildlife and would know what a prairie lark was and how it lived. She knew Sarah would understand.

Be looking for analogies in books, magazines, people's conversations, radio, etc., to point out to your student.

Language Arts: Imagery—Sarah's Voice

At the end of our chapter, in Anna's journal entry we read her description of Sarah's words, "...even her words were like a song" (page 42). What does your student think that means? Does he think Sarah's voice actually lilts when she speaks, like a song?

For discussion, your student might examine this possibility. Often, song lyrics use a lot of imagery. Imagery is a literary term meaning words or phrases which include comparisons and vivid description. For example, "the sunset as red as a robin's breast." Or, "her eyes spoke a thousand words, like throngs of angry people." Imagery is used in poetry and literature of all sorts, and sometimes people employ beautiful imagery in their speech.

When Sarah speaks, her words are full of images. Look back on just a few of her phrases from the first book and *Skylark*:

"But I've touched seals. Real seals. They are cool and slippery and they slide through the water like fish." *(Sarah, page 26)*

"The sea is salt. It stretches out as far as you can see. It gleams like the sun on glass. There are waves." (*Sarah*, page 37)

"What was between the lines?" Caleb asked... "His life," she said simply. (*Skylark*, page 11)

So, perhaps when Anna described Sarah's words as a song, this is what she meant—the use of imagery and poetic devices.

Fine Arts: Cooking—Biscuits

The beginning of our chapter finds Sarah mixing up biscuit batter (page 36). Biscuits were a staple during pioneer times. These quick bread products were easy and quick to make, not requiring any time for rising like yeast breads.

If your student likes to cook, perhaps this would be a good opportunity to take some time and bake. Here is one recipe for biscuits, but if you have a favorite, by all means, use that.

Biscuits—Like Sarah Might Have Made

1 3/4 cups all-purpose flour
1 tsp. salt
2 tsp. baking powder
1 tsp. sugar
1/2 tsp. soda
1/4 cup cold butter or margarine
2/3 cup buttermilk

Sift together flour, salt, baking powder, sugar and soda. Cut in butter or margarine. Add buttermilk. After very lightly mixing, turn the dough onto a floured board. Knead it very lightly for 1 minute. Pat the dough into a flat circle approximately 2" thick. Cut into circles with either a biscuit cutter or the floured rim of a drinking glass. Bake at 450° F. for 10-12 minutes. Enjoy!

Writing and Discussion Question

Sarah and Caleb discussed the difference between a daydream and a night dream (page 36). How would you describe the difference? What is a daydream you have often? Write or talk about it.

Vocabulary Word

analogy: a story or example which helps simplify a more complex story

Internet Connections

To view current suggested links relating to this chapter's lessons, see www.fiveinarow.com/connections.

Chapter 8

Parent Summary

A lone, starved coyote comes to drink from the Wittings' well and Papa must shoot it. Sarah, completely devastated by seeing the animal put down, retreats to be alone. Fortunately, Sarah's birthday arrives and the festivities cheer everyone up. Her aunts from Maine send her a phonograph. Papa and Sarah dance. By the end of the day, Sarah is feeling much happier.

What we will cover in this chapter:

History and Geography: The Phonograph—An Edison Invention

Science: Shade—A Scarce Commodity on the Prairie

Language Arts: Book Recommendation—*What You Know First*

Language Arts: Author's License—Breaking the Rules on Purpose

Issues of Human Relationships:
Making Instead of Buying—Giving Precious Gifts

Lesson Activities

History and Geography: The Phonograph—An Edison Invention

Sarah's aunts from Maine are very kind to send her such a wonderful birthday present—a phonograph (page 47)! Imagine, being isolated on the prairie and suddenly having the gift of music. If your student studied Thomas Alva Edison in *Beyond Five in a Row*, Volume 1, he might remember that Edison developed the first working phonograph in 1877.

Edison's first model of the phonograph, although somewhat crude, is still quite similar to the record players of today. They all operate by the principle of sound being a vibration. Edison had someone speak (or sing) into a funnel-like mouthpiece and the person's voice vibrations were then recorded by a needle on a piece of tin foil. To replay the speech or song, Edison placed another needle on the same piece of grooved tin, which had been wrapped around a cylinder tube. When the tube was turned and the needle passed along the grooves and was amplified, the sounds could be heard.

Later on, in 1887, Emile Berliner, a German inventor living in America, improved the invention further. Instead of tin or metal cylinders, he created discs coated in shellac [sha LACK—a varnish made from alcohol which creates a very smooth and shiny finish to wood, metal or plastic]. Not only did Berliner's new "records" provide clearer sound, but they were easier to mass-produce for sale. The earliest models of phonographs became available by 1925.

If there is interest, more study can be done on the history of the phonograph. It might also be useful to review past lessons on Edison from *Beyond Five in a Row*, Volume 1.

Science: Shade—A Scarce Commodity on the Prairie

Draw your student's attention to the following line located on page 47—"Outside there was a table in the shade of the house, set with food and lemonade." Now, remind your student of a similar sentence from our first study, *Sarah, Plain and Tall*, on page 39—"...then they set up a big table in the shade of the barn..."

If your student were going to give a picnic outside on tables, where would he think to put the tables and chairs? One common response might be—under the trees. Certainly, if it were summertime and hot, shade would be what you were looking for and trees do seem like the logical spot, don't they? However, remind your student of where our story takes place. Sarah, Papa and the children live on the prairie. Generally, prairies do not have many trees, if any. For the Wittings and their guests, the only spot for shade is under the eaves of the house or barn.

For very similar reasons, due to the heat, drought and lack of shade, having a lawn was obviously difficult as well. On page 48 we read, "Everyone danced, then, in the dirt yard..." Does your student have a lawn? What would it be like to have a front yard of only dust and soil? It would certainly be different.

If possible, go outside with your student and sit or stand under a tree's shade and enjoy!

Language Arts: Book Recommendation—*What You Know First*

Patricia MacLachlan, our author, is a wonderful writer. Many of the things she remembers from her childhood have influenced her books, and if you read them carefully, you'll see similar themes used again and again. For example, look with your student at page 49 and read the final lines from Anna's journal—Sarah's birthday gift.

"My mother, Sarah, doesn't love the prairie. She tries, but she can't help remembering what she knew first."

MacLachlan used this same sentiment as a title and theme for a different book, published a year after *Skylark*. If your student is enjoying *Sarah, Plain and Tall* and *Skylark*, please try to locate another MacLachlan title, *What You Know First* (Copyright 1995, Joanna Cotler Books, ISBN 0060244135).

Written with the same creativity and integrity MacLachlan is hailed for, this book is a delightful supplement to your *Sarah* studies. The illustrations are breathtaking. Barry Moser, a National Book Award-winning artist, selected (with the help of MacLachlan) old photographs of their own families. Then, by using a synthetic wood medium, he created engravings of the photographs, made blocks and then printed them. The result is magnificent.

This book is highly recommended for anyone, young or old. It is another MacLachlan treasure.

Language Arts:
Author's License—Breaking the Rules on Purpose

If you feel your student has a firm enough comprehension of basic grammar and sentence structure, this lesson offers an interesting introduction to author's license. Sometimes writers (particularly in poetry and fiction) make exceptions to basic grammatical rules. In this chapter we see MacLachlan writing in this way on page 48. She writes, "For a while, everyone was happy again. Even Sarah. Even Papa."

Ask your student if the last two sentences are really sentences? No, they are not. To be complete and grammatically sound, a sentence must include a subject and a verb.

These sentences are lacking a verb. Ask your student why he thinks MacLachlan uses these odd, short sentences at the end of her paragraph?

Perhaps she wanted to draw attention to those two characters—Sarah and Papa. When you read that section, an emphasis is obviously on those two phrases.

Authors and poets sometimes break other grammatical rules on purpose. For example, the famous American poet, E. E. Cummings, often did not make use of capital letters or punctuation of any kind. (He even wrote his own name: e.e.cummings.) Born in 1894 (died in 1962), Cummings' full name was Edward Estlin Cummings. His poetry is famous for its lack of traditional sentence structure, his abandonment of proper syntax, his purposeful disregard for punctuation and capitalization, and his wild and fanciful experiments with typography (the arrangement of the words on the page).

Here is an example of e.e.cummings' work:

In Just –

in Just –
spring when the world is mud-
luscious the little
lame balloonman
whistles   far   and wee

and edieandbill come
running from marbles and
piracies and it's
spring

when the world is puddle-wonderful

the queer
old balloonman whistles
far   and   wee
and bettyandisbel come dancing

from hop-scotch and jump-rope and

it's
spring
and
          the
                    goat-footed
balloonMan   whistles
far
and
wee

Another striking example of Cummings' creativity with letters and shapes is found in the first line of another poem, which is:

"mOOn Over tOwns mOOn"

Cummings has made the observation that the letter "o" resembles the moon. To emphasize this point, he breaks the rules of punctuation and exaggerates the letters "o" by placing them in capital form.

If your student enjoys creative writing, either in fiction, journal writing, or poetry, perhaps he would like to experiment with his own creative "license"—by making simple changes, as subtle as MacLachlan, or wild changes like that of E. E. Cummings.

Issues of Human Relationships:
Making Instead of Buying—Giving Precious Gifts

Anna gave Sarah a precious birthday gift—something she had written herself (page 48). Anna's journal for her mother includes her own thoughts and feelings—herself. Sometimes, the gifts we make for others mean more to them than those we buy. Has your student ever made his own present for someone? What was it? What gave him the idea? Did it take more work than buying something? Was it worth it? Did the recipient appreciate the extra time and love? Or has your student ever received a gift which was hand-created just for him?

Often the value of a gift is not dependent upon how much it cost. Instead, it is based more in the love it took to make it. Encourage your student to try to make a gift for a friend or family member soon. Just like Anna, he too can give precious gifts.

Writing and Discussion Question

Caleb's glass disappears from its resting spot on the fence post (page 50). Sarah notices this and asks Jacob to put it back. Why do you think Caleb's rain glass was gone? Who took it down? Why?

Vocabulary Words

shellac: a varnish made from alcohol which creates a very smooth and shiny finish

license: freedom of action, speech or thought

Internet Connections

To view current suggested links relating to this chapter's lessons, see www.fiveinarow.com/connections.

Chapter 9

Parent Summary

Just as things were beginning to get a little brighter, Maggie and Matthew's well runs dry. They are forced to move. Having her neighbors and only close woman friend leaving is difficult for Sarah. That night, Anna is awakened by a clap of thunder. Lightening strikes the barn and a fire begins to rage. No matter how many buckets of water they collect and pour on the flames, the Wittings cannot stop it. The family stands and watches their barn burn to the ground. The next day a major decision is reached. The drought has become too severe. Sarah, Anna and Caleb will move back to Maine and stay with the aunts until it is over. Papa will not go with them because he must watch over the land.

What we will cover in this chapter:

History and Geography: Wells—A Brief Overview

Science: Watertable—What It Is and How to Create Your Own

Issues of Human Relationships: Dealing With Hard Choices

Lesson Activities

History and Geography: Wells—A Brief Overview

On page 51 we learn Maggie and Matthew are being forced to move from their home on the prairie. Their well has run dry. The Wittings and their neighbors obviously rely on their wells as the primary source of water. Does your student live in a rural area where people still use wells? Has he ever thought about where his own water comes from?

Why not take some time and explore with your student the topic of wells. Throughout history, wells have been gathering places of the community. In some smaller villages in Africa, South America and Europe the town well was not only the place for collecting the family's water supply each day, but it was also the "information post"—the place where the men and women in the village discussed civic matters, family life and social events.

There is one basic definition of a well. A well is a hole in the ground from which water (or oil or natural gases) can be withdrawn. The water that is taken from a well (just like Sarah and Jacob's) is known as ground water. This water is present in the ground generally from rain soaking down through the crust of the earth. The water is contained in the soil and the permeable and semi-permeable bedrock.

But how does a person find the area in the ground where a well is present? Highly trained geologists and engineers make this their careers. They can find where the water is located and then, through the use of special equipment, they are able to determine where to drill or dig, how much water can be removed without destroying the natural resources, and at what rate.

In pioneer days, men and women simply observed their surroundings and attempted to determine where water would be most likely found. At times this was a matter of guesswork—a matter of trial and error.

If your student is interested in learning more about wells, additional topics suitable for study are: artesian wells, oil and gas wells, seismographs and mineral wells.

Science: Watertable—What It Is and How to Create Your Own

Matthew and Maggie's well ran dry. Why? Where did the water go? When someone digs a well, isn't there always going to be water in it?

To answer these questions and to have a better understanding of geology, discuss with your student the subject of watertables.

A watertable is the scientific term for the surface of ground water—the top level. Below the watertable is the water source and above it is the earth. In certain areas (flood plains are a good example), the soil is so highly saturated (soaked) in water, the watertable is very close to the surface. When heavy rains fall, the watertable rises (sometimes above the level of the ground) and floods occur. The soil cannot absorb or hold any more water. Conversely, in dryer areas (much like that of the prairie where the Wittings live) the watertable is low and then in times of drought, drops even further down. This is what causes wells to run dry.

To illustrate this point for your student, help him create his own mini-watertable. Take a clear drinking glass or mason jar and have him fill it 2/3 full, with small stones, gravel, or even marbles.

[**Teacher's Note**: Sand or soil may be used for this experiment, but the rate of evaporation will be much slower. If pebbles or marbles are used, the results can be seen in just a day or two.]

After the glass is filled with your student's "earth," fill the jar with water. Your student can observe how the water filtrates down and surrounds the pebbles, and then begins to fill above them and creates a clear water reservoir. (A reservoir is a place where water (or another substance) is collected and stored for use.) Now, have your student mark on the side of the jar where the watertable (or surface) is located.

Help your student place a small straw (or one cut in half) on the inside of the jar and tape it to the side (place it where you can see the bottom of the straw easily). Don't put the straw all the way to the bottom of the jar and marbles—instead, only about a third of the way down. This straw is now your student's well. What does he think will happen? If every time a little water evaporated, he continued to replenish the supply (in the way rain and rivers would under normal conditions) then his straw would always be submerged in the water. But what if a drought occurred? To illustrated this, encourage your student to leave the jar in a sunny window (or even outside) overnight. Has the water level gone down at all? How about in one day? In two days? How long does it take before the watertable is below the bottom of the straw? What happens then? If no more water is put into the "earth," no water can be drawn out. Sure, you could dig the well deeper. But then what? This is the dilemma which faces Maggie and Matthew. When a well runs dry, people begin to panic. Without water, people die.

When people like the Wittings dug a well, they would generally dig a good number of feet down past the watertable. Then, in case of a dry spell, they would have some leverage and still be able to access water. But when a drought occurs and the watertable drops below where the well can reach, that is when you say, the well has "run dry."

Understanding watertables and the way ground saturation affects our supply of water is fundamental to understanding flood plains and droughts. Nature has created for us a delicate balance of resources and it is important to learn how to conserve and share those resources to our best advantage.

If your student is interested in learning more about watertables, good topics of discussion are dams, geology, water conservation and water pollution.

Issues of Human Relationships: Dealing With Hard Choices

Reread with your student the first few sentences on page 55:

"I saw her shake her head, no. I saw Papa take her hand. She shook her head again. Then Papa put his arms around her. I knew we would have to go away."

Sarah and the children don't want to leave Papa and go to Maine. Leaving the prairie, leaving Nick and Lottie and Seal, and most of all, leaving Papa will be difficult and sad. Certainly watching Maggie, Matthew and the children being forced to leave their home was an incentive for Jacob to come up with a plan. The Wittings don't want to lose their home entirely. If Sarah and the children can live in Maine for awhile, then there will probably be enough water for Jacob and the animals alone. He can also keep an eye on his land and watch for any more fires.

Sometimes it is necessary in life to deal with hard choices. Has your student ever had to make a difficult decision? What were the circumstances? What did he decide? There is an old saying, "You're between a rock and a hard place." Ask your student what he thinks that means. It is a play on words—rocks are hard places. Using this phrase is like saying you are between a hard place and a hard place. It's a way of describing a tough situation. It means there is no easy answer.

For Sarah, staying on the farm with Anna and Caleb could be dangerous for all of them. But leaving Jacob and returning to her former home for a season is going to be painful, too. How does a person decide what's best? In the end, Sarah probably had to rely on two things. First, she understands that going back to Maine is the safest thing for the children. Secondly, she trusts Jacob. He thinks they should leave and so she listens.

Learning to weigh issues and compare pros and cons is one way people deal with difficult decisions. Sometimes it results in picking the option that's the 'least' painful—but hard, nonetheless. Sometimes, being in tough situations means we may need to listen to others and what they say—people we trust to steer us in the right direction.

Encourage your student to think about what making a difficult choice involves—how people think and what they can do to arrive at a decision. It is a sign of maturity when people are able to face tough problems with grace and commitment to a solution, instead of folding under the pressure.

Writing and Discussion Question

Jacob and Sarah have their discussion about leaving the prairie in private (page 54). Anna watches them talking, but she doesn't hear anything they are saying. How do you think that conversation went? What do you think Papa might have said to convince Sarah to go? What do you think Sarah might have said in disagreement?

Vocabulary Words

well: a hole in the ground from which water (or oil or natural gases) can be withdrawn

ground water: water held beneath the earth's surface

reservoir: a place where water is stored and collected for use

watertable: the level below which the ground is saturated with water

Internet Connections

To view current suggested links relating to this chapter's lessons, see www.fiveinarow.com/connections.

Chapter 10

Parent Summary

Sarah, Anna, and Caleb travel for three days by train to Maine. They travel the same route Sarah had taken to come out to the prairie to live with them. When they arrive at the train station in Maine, they are met by an old friend who takes them by car to Sarah's aunts' home. Aunts Mattie, Harriet, and Lou love the children and are thrilled to have Sarah back. By the end of the evening, Anna begins to cry as she remembers how much she's already missing her father.

What we will cover in this chapter:

History and Geography: Maine—Learning More about This State

History and Geography: A Clue to *Skylark's* Time Frame—The Automobile

Science: Tides and Oceans

Fine Arts: Julius Caesar and Aunt Lou's Dog

Issues of Human Relationships:
Being a Part of a Family—Understanding More About Sarah

Lesson Activities

History and Geography: Maine—Learning More about This State

Anna and Caleb are in Maine—Sarah's birthplace and home (page 58). It must be very different from the prairie. The first observation of this new place we see is on page 58. "Maine was *green*."

If you did an introductory lesson on the state of Maine from this volume, chapter 1 in *Sarah, Plain and Tall*, your student may already have a basic understanding of this interesting northeastern region. However, for more detailed information on Maine, you might wish to take some time and do more in-depth research with your student.

Your local library may have good books about Maine. Try to locate a travel video about this state and look for additional tourism information. You might even locate a Maine newspaper on file or on microfiche for additional study.

To make it more interesting, give your student an imaginary mission of some kind. For example, tell him you need to find an area to live in Maine where you will get the best view of the ocean or the most forest behind your house, or the quickest access to Boston or New York. Perhaps he enjoys snow skiing or snowmobiling—where would he go for these activities? What's Maine's southern-most city? What's the northern-most city?

By setting goals for research, your student will learn a great deal about this state and will have fun at the same time.

History and Geography: A Clue to *Skylark's* Time Frame—The Automobile

Up to this point in our story, we could only guess at a general time frame for our tale. MacLachlan never gives us a year or date for our characters. When does your student think this story takes place? What clues can we gather? How do we determine a time frame?

One good way to judge roughly when a story takes place is to look at the technology and industry mentioned. Sarah and Jacob do not drive an automobile, but instead, a horse and buggy. However, Sarah did arrive on the prairie via train. In *Skylark*, chapter 10, we see Chub arriving to pick the Wittings up in a car (page 59). Caleb comments, "I've never been in a car before." If cars were already in the east, but not the west, then it must have been a fairly new invention.

Henry Ford, born in 1863 in Dearborn, Michigan, invented the first gasoline powered engine in 1893—his first automobile in 1896. After working for several years at the Detroit Electric Company, Ford (at the age of 40) organized the Ford Motor Company. The company developed the first car for family consumers and called it the 'Model T.' These affordable and surprisingly reliable cars were available for sale in 1908. By 1913, they were fairly common on the east coast.

From this information, we can deduce that our story of the Wittings probably took place not long after the turn of the 20th century—perhaps between 1905 and 1915. Caleb didn't seem shocked by the concept of an automobile—he didn't say he had never heard of or seen one. He just said he had never ridden in one.

For more study and enriched lessons, your student can now take this approximate time frame and begin doing outside research into the life and times of the Wittings. Who was President? (William Howard Taft served as President from 1909-1913. President Taft is the only U.S. president to serve first as President and then as Chief Justice.) What was the favorite sport? (Baseball, which had been introduced by Northern soldiers to the South during the Civil War (1861-65), was now so popular it became known as the national pastime.) What was the music of the time? (The most popular music was called ragtime, evolving from old-time military marches. This highly syncopated music became the rage from 1895-1915. The most famous ragtime piece was written by Scott Joplin (1899) and was called "Maple Leaf Rag." Joplin was called the 'King of Ragtime.') Find some examples of recorded ragtime music and listen. Libraries often have music to borrow.

Share these bits of information with your student and encourage him to find many more. This time in history was fascinating. Understanding more about it helps us to flesh out our understanding of the Wittings and their life. Remind your student that it is from these kinds of clues that we are often able to decipher the time frame of a story.

Science: Tides and Oceans

In this chapter, Caleb and Anna get their first peek at the great Atlantic Ocean. Caleb's first remark is an excellent description. He merely says, "All that water!" (page 59). Can you imagine how amazed the children must have been to see the ocean, after living on the prairie all their life? And after being in a drought? What a shock it must have been. On page 63, in Anna's journal entry we read her observations, "...the tide going in and going out, the moon rising above the water."

Why not take this opportunity to share with your student more information on the oceans of the world? You can even do some exploration into ocean tides and how they are patterned.

To begin, the term 'ocean' is used to describe the single massive body of water that covers 70% of the earth's surface. This body of water is often referred to as the 'global ocean' or 'world ocean.' To make it more specific, however, scientists have broken this body of water into four smaller oceans. They are, from largest to smallest: Pacific Ocean, Atlantic Ocean, Indian Ocean and the Arctic Ocean (occasionally called the Arctic Sea). The average depth of the ocean is 12,000 feet, but many areas are much deeper.

By looking at a map or globe, locate these bodies of water with your student and compare each. As we learned from Sarah in *Sarah, Plain and Tall* (page 36), the sea is salt water. Seawater, on average, contains 3 1/2% salt. The wildlife found in an ocean is different from the animal life anywhere else in the world. If there is interest, take some time and let your student explore one or two interesting sea creatures (for example: anemones, jellyfish, manta rays and starfish).

The water in an ocean moves in tides. These rising and falling movements in the water are on a very specific time schedule. Some cultures that live along an ocean coast tell time by the tides. Tides follow the motion of the moon as it orbits the earth. According to researchers, the tides rise and fall twice in the time between two rising moons, 24 hours and 50 minutes. As the earth turns on its axis, the moon appears to move across the sky about once a day. The gravity of the moon's rotation pulls the water in each ocean away from the solid ground on one side of the earth, and on the opposite side of the planet, the gravity of the moon is pulling the earth away from the waters. These two pulls from opposite sides of the earth produce a hump of water, and these are the positions of high tide.

If you are fortunate enough to live near the ocean, take your student for a day trip soon. Examine wildlife and fascinating plants, and observe low and high tide. This field trip can provide your student with hands-on exploration and enrich his studies.

If you do not live near an ocean, find some books at your local library or bookstore that have photographs of marine life and the oceans of the world. Look for good videos at your library. If you can't see something in person, a beautiful full-color photograph or video can be the next best thing!

Fine Arts: Julius Caesar and Aunt Lou's Dog

Does your student remember what Aunt Lou's dog is named? Brutus (page 61). What an interesting name. Take some time and explore with your student Marcus Brutus, Julius Caesar and even some information about Shakespeare's interpretation of the historic assassination involving these two figures.

Julius Caesar (100?-44 B.C.) was one of the most famous and powerful Roman statesmen and leaders of ancient times. He was a renowned orator (a speech giver) and philosopher whom many compared to Cicero (the most recognized orator, writer and philosopher of the day). Caesar won many battles and was appointed the dictator (ruler) of Rome. He was a charismatic and fearless man, and his people loved him as much as his enemies hated him.

One of Caesar's chief administrators and generals was a man named Marcus Brutus [BROO tuhs]. In a fascinating turn of events, Brutus, who had been fighting on behalf of Pompey (Caesar's political rival—the last man who stood in the way of Caesar's rise to power), was appointed by Caesar to align with Rome. Pompey was defeated mercilessly and killed, and Brutus came to fight for Caesar. However, Brutus never truly trusted Caesar and was frightened by the love of power that he displayed. Brutus did not want Caesar to be king.

Caesar considered Brutus a friend. He worked and spent social time with Brutus every day. He trusted him. Brutus was jealous of the power Caesar was gaining. On March 15, 44 B.C., with the encouragement and help of the Roman General Cassius, Brutus led a march to kill Caesar. Brutus, along with several other men, stabbed their leader to death on his way to a Roman Senate building. The great Julius Caesar was dead.

Throughout history, since this terrible event, the name Brutus has been used much like the name of Benedict Arnold—as a term for a traitor. If your student is interest, William Shakespeare wrote of this amazing event in one of his 'history' plays. The now-famous literary line, synonymous with friends turning on friends and political overthrow "Et tu, Brute?" is Latin for "And you, Brutus?"

If your student is interested in great historical events, politics, military stories or Shakespeare, take some time to read the play *Julius Caesar* by William Shakespeare. It might prove to be a wonderful enrichment lesson. The beauty of the language and the story are both stunning.

Issues of Human Relationships: Being a Part of a Family—Understanding More About Sarah

From our story, we understand that Sarah is not a very 'conventional' woman of the early 1900s. Ask your student what he can remember from our first book, *Sarah, Plain and Tall*, that would give him any clues. Sarah wore Papa's overalls. She helped him fix the roof. She let her chickens run around in the house. Remember what Jacob said (page 55)? "Sarah is Sarah. She does things her way, you know."

Then, in this story, we are allowed to meet her aunts from Maine—Mattie, Harriet and Lou. Just as Sarah mentioned before, the aunts wear silk dresses around the house and no shoes (page 60). That's unconventional! And her Aunt Lou wears overalls and high boots, and works with animals—she doesn't like silk and pearls.

What can we learn from these delightful character sketches? When we grow up, we will never be "just like" our parents or a grandparent. We are a product of our mother, father and our ancestors. However, sometimes, the way we are raised dictates to a degree the way we turn out. Sarah is unconventional, but now we see her aunts are as well. 'Meeting' her family helps us understand Sarah better, doesn't it?

[**Teacher's Note**: Remind your student that when he writes his own stories, he can develop his characters by showing how both people and events have influenced their lives.]

What does your student see in himself that reminds him of a parent? What does he notice about his interests or characteristics that are different?

Writing and Discussion Question

On page 58 we read, "When we got off the train, Sarah stood still. She looked at the train station, and at the trees, and at the people… 'It's all right, Anna,' said Sarah. 'It's just what you wrote in your book. I've come back to what I knew first.'"

What do you think Sarah was thinking about as she looked around her? Does she miss Maine, or is she thinking of Papa back on the prairie? Is she sad, happy, or a combination? Describe what you think Sarah's thoughts are like.

Vocabulary Words

> **global ocean**: the ocean waters as a single body of water, worldwide

> **tides**: the rise and fall of the ocean, approximately every twelve hours, due
> to the movement of the sun and moon in relation to the earth

Internet Connections

To view current suggested links relating to this chapter's lessons, see www.fiveinarow.com/connections.

Chapter 11

Parent Summary

The days stretch into weeks as Anna, Caleb and Sarah stay in Maine. The children miss their father more and more, and the letter writing grows more frequent. One day, Sarah has her brother take her to see the doctor. She won't tell the children what the doctor said, but she assures them she's not sick.

Papa writes and tells them that Seal had her kittens—three gray and one orange. Caleb and Anna begin to wonder if the drought will ever end—will they ever go back to Papa and the prairie?

What we will cover in this chapter:

Language Arts: Developing Symmetry in Your Writing

Fine Arts: "Hush, Little Baby"—The Song

Lesson Activities

Language Arts: Developing Symmetry in Your Writing

When we began our story, reading *Sarah, Plain and Tall*, the story was framed by letters from Sarah to the Wittings. We learned information about Sarah and the other characters and were able to follow the story through the letters, just as Anna, Caleb and Papa did.

Now, in *Skylark*, we find Anna, Caleb and Sarah in Maine, writing letters back and forth to Papa. Our author, Patricia MacLachlan, has done a wonderful job of creating symmetry within her story. Symmetry is a word that means balance or equality—to arrange two things evenly and opposite one another.

When we write stories, it is interesting to try to achieve symmetry in a variety of ways within the story. Perhaps at the beginning of your story a character makes a specific statement, and then that same sentiment is repeated at the end of the story. Or a description of the sky or an animal is used throughout the story, again and again. Here, in the *Sarah* books, we can observe a subtle, but delightful symmetry in the way MacLachlan uses the postal letters.

Noticing symmetry or balance in stories allows us to more fully appreciate the thought and skill the author used when writing them. Encourage your student to try developing symmetry today in one of his own stories.

Fine Arts: "Hush, Little Baby"—The Song

Sarah comforts Anna and Caleb with a song (page 70). It is an old lullaby, entitled "Hush, Little Baby." The song centers around presents being offered by the parent to the baby, one by one. Even if the presents don't last, the song seems to say the love of the parent will always be there.

If your student plays the piano or flute, perhaps the music located at the back of this book can be helpful. If you remember the song's tune, sing it along with your student today. It is delightful lullaby. Here are the full lyrics:

"Hush, Little Baby"

Hush, little baby, don't say a word.
Papa's gonna buy you a mockingbird.
And if that mockingbird don't sing,
Papa's gonna buy you a diamond ring.

And if that diamond ring turns to brass
Papa's gonna buy you a looking glass.
And if that looking glass gets broke,
Papa's gonna buy you a billy goat.

And if that billy goat won't pull,
Papa's gonna buy you a cart and bull.
And if that cart and bull turn over,
Papa's gonna buy you a dog named Rover.

And if that dog named Rover won't bark,
Papa's gonna buy you a horse and cart.
And if that horse and cart fall down,
You'll still be the sweetest little baby in town.

Writing and Discussion Question

Why do you think Sarah went to see the doctor. What's going on?

Vocabulary Word

symmetry: balanced; opposite sides which are equal

Internet Connections

To view current suggested links relating to this chapter's lessons, see www.fiveinarow.com/connections.

Chapter 12

Parent Summary

Anna and Caleb wake up to the sound of rain beating down. They haven't heard that sound in a long time. Sarah, Anna, Caleb and even William dance and jump and laugh in the rain. When Anna writes her father a letter that night, she does not tell him about the rain.

Later that evening, the three aunts drink tea under the moon. Caleb gets to know Aunt Harriet better, and Aunt Lou goes skinny-dipping. Anna sits and wonders if Sarah is missing Maine even more, now that she's back. The children hope they can return home soon.

What we will cover in this chapter:

Science: Water Safety

Science: Loon—An Interesting Bird

Fine Arts: Special Occasions—Setting Up a Moonlight Tea

Lesson Activities

Science: Water Safety

Draw your student's attention to page 75 and the following sentence—*"The bell buoy made a lonely, sad sound."* Does your student know what a buoy is? Why is it called a bell buoy? A buoy is just one device people employ to make the coastal and lake waters safe. Take this learning opportunity to share with your student some of the fascinating technology and equipment people use to guide their ships and their crews.

A buoy [pronounced two ways: BOY or BOO ee] is an anchored object which floats on top of the water and helps guide ships. The buoys work a little like lines on a road—showing the captain and crew where the safe area of water is located, in order to dock or pass through a narrow inlet. Buoys are designed in different colors and shapes. For example, in the United States, red buoys are used to designate the right side of a channel. In other countries the color green is used. Buoys with an orange diamond on a white background show ships where dangerous waters are located. Some buoys are cone-shaped, cylindrical or even spheres.

Like the buoy in our story, some buoys have bells, lights, whistles or other sounding/sighting devices. The sounding buoys help ships during fog—when they cannot see colors or lights.

Buoys are only one means ships use to navigate through the water. Maps are essential tools for captains and their crews. A map for a ship or boat is called a chart or nautical chart. Oceanographers and cartographers (people who create maps) use tools and special equipment to create the charts. Nautical charts are often updated every year—making note of changes in reefs, sandbars, underwater mountains, islands, etc. Charts are vital for a ship's safe passage. You and your student might enjoy reading *We Didn't Mean to Go to Sea* by Arthur Ransome. Check with your local library for this or any of the other books in the Swallows and Amazons series by Ransome.

Lighthouses are another way ships are able to navigate safely. Even 100 years ago, lighthouses were depended upon heavily by navigators because they allowed them to see the edges of piers, ports and shore. As technology has advanced, however, new electronic navigation systems have been developed—using radio signals to determine the ship's course. In the early 1900s (the time of our story), there were over 1,500 lighthouses operating in the United States. Today, there are only a little over 300, and only 1,400 in the entire world. These lighthouses used to be operated and maintained by people—they even lived in the lighthouse all the time. They checked the lamps, cleaned the glass and prevented vandalism. Today, however, the few lighthouses left are operated automatically, with no need of human assistance.

If your student is interested in this discussion, he may wish to do additional research on any of the topics mentioned above. Another excellent subject for research is the electronic navigation methods. 'Loran,' for example, is the name of the method used in the United States. Loran stands for long range navigation. 'Loran-C' is the system used in Canada. These two systems use highly technical transmitting devices and radio signals. Although this topic is complex, your student may want to explore it.

Another great way to enrich your student's understanding of ship navigation is to locate a good chart from a local map or bookstore. Let him look at the legend, the directional signals and the complex nature of the chart. To guide a ship safely to dock, sailors must have a grounded understanding of charts and the waters that they navigate. (Again, an enjoyable way to learn about charts, navigation and lighthouses is to read the delightful stories of Arthur Ransome.)

Science: Loon—An Interesting Bird

Anna hears the cry of a loon (page 75). Does your student know what a loon is? Has he ever seen one? Take some time to explore this interesting animal with your student.

The loon is a water bird that swims and dives. He has a long, sleek body and a sharp, pointed bill that is used to catch fish for food. When the loon swims in the water, he looks like a very large duck. Unlike ducks, however, instead of just bobbing beneath the water's surface for food, the loon can dive to deep depths in search of food.

The loon is the state bird of Minnesota, but can be seen all along the Northern United States. Common loons have black bodies with white spots. There are also the yellow-billed loon, the Arctic loon and the red-throated loon.

The loon's call is quite unusual. They have a slight maniacal, raucous laughing voice. Their bizarre "laughter" is the basis for the old saying, "crazy as a loon." The Canadian dollar coin has a loon engraved on one side of it. The Canadians call them 'loonies.' And the two-dollar coins are called 'twoonies.'

Locate a nice photograph of a loon for your student—and share with him the beautiful bird Anna and Caleb were able to see. If you have a student who loves drawing, have him carefully draw a loon from a wildlife picture or encyclopedia.

Fine Arts: Special Occasions—Setting Up a Moonlight Tea

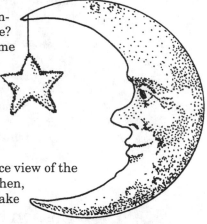

Sarah's aunts serve tea under the moonlight (page 73). What a wonderful idea! If your student would enjoy it, why not plan a late night tea time? If your student likes to cook this could be an opportunity to let him bake some special cookies, biscuits or sandwiches. And, of course, tea is only necessary if that is something everyone likes. Aunt Harriet, Mattie and Lou preferred tea, but you could serve lemonade, soda pop or cocoa if that would be more to your student's liking. Allow your student to help with as much of the preparations as he wishes—this can be an enjoyable exercise in planning as well.

Spread a big blanket on a grassy patch, and make sure you have a nice view of the moon. Pillows can be taken out, if you want to lay back and look at the sky. Then, under the stars, chat with your student about whatever comes to mind. Make this a special, sparkling event—something to be remembered for a lifetime!

Writing and Discussion Question

Anna describes the fireworks they see from far away: "They're like the dandelions that bloom in the fields at home in summer" (page 75). How would you describe the designs of fireworks against a night sky? What would you compare them to?

Vocabulary Words

buoy: an object in water which is anchored and then floats, may have bells, whistles, or lights attached

chart: a map used on ships

Loran/Loran-C: the names of the long range navigational devices used in the United States and Canada

Internet Connections

To view current suggested links relating to this chapter's lessons, see www.fiveinarow.com/connections.

Chapters 13-15

[**Teacher's Note**: Due to the brevity of the last three chapters in *Skylark*, the lessons have been combined as a single lesson plan. As you finish the remaining lessons, take some time to reflect on this unit and explore any lessons you may have missed or wish to complete.]

Parent Summary

Caleb and Sarah begin to doubt whether or not they will return to the prairie. Even Sarah doesn't seem to know when. Caleb loses interest in fishing and Brutus and begins to become very sad. Anna finds him one night crying near a cove by the house. He wants to go home.

The following day, Papa arrives in Maine! He has surprised everyone. It rained on the prairie and he has come for them. The children cry and laugh, and Sarah is happy. That night Papa and Sarah tell the children they are expecting a new baby—this is why Sarah had made that trip to the doctor. Sarah assures Anna she is healthy and the baby will be okay. She knows Anna is frightened because of what happened to her first mother, when she gave birth to Caleb.

Finally, after many long weeks, the Wittings arrive home on the prairie. Caleb runs and greets the dogs. The children laugh at Seal's new kittens. The family enjoys being together again. In the spring, they will have a new baby to call their own.

What we will cover in these chapters:

History and Geography: Completing Your Sea and Prairie Notebooks

Science: Genetics—Simple Beginning Lessons

Language Arts: Creative Writing—The Wittings One Year Later

Issues of Human Relationships: Working Through Fears

Lesson Activities

History and Geography:
Completing Your Sea and Prairie Notebooks

If your student has been maintaining Sea and Prairie Notebooks throughout these last two units, now would be a great time to finish that project. This chapter offers a few more "notes" for the journals—lobster traps, coves and buoys.

Perhaps your student would like to decorate the outside of his notebooks. Quotes from the story, drawn or painted pictures of sea or prairie scenes, even a picture of his favorite character would make excellent 'cover' art.

When your student has finished his project, he can show and discuss it with his family, grandparents or friends. He may even wish to keep adding to one or both if he is interested in continued study on a specific topic. For example, prairie grasses, fishing, ships or droughts.

Encourage your student to file his notebooks away carefully. They will provide excellent review materials later on in his school year, and will be an enjoyable reminder of his time spent with these two Patricia MacLachlan books.

Science: Genetics—Simple Beginning Lessons

Seal is a gray cat and Sam, Maggie's cat, is orange. Draw your student's attention to page 85 and the description of Seal's new kittens: "three colored gray and one with an orange coat." Does your student know why that happens? If a parent has blue eyes, will all of his/her children have blue eyes? What determines which characteristics are passed on?

Share with your student a simple introduction to the world of genetics. A characteristic, such as blue eyes, small ears or gray fur, is called a trait. Traits are revealed in our bodies through our genes. It is from the word 'gene' that we get the word 'genetics.' Traits can be things we see (like hair color and foot size) or they can be things inside our bodies (like allergies or mental capacities). When we talk about traits, two words are used to describe them—dominant and recessive.

A dominant trait is one which, when put up against any other, will always show itself. It is the 'stronger' trait. A recessive trait will be masked, unless the genes it is represented by are all recessive. For example, three of Seal's kittens were gray. Gray is obviously the dominant color trait. The kittens that have gray fur either had all dominant genes, or an equal number of each—dominant and recessive. Only the kitten that had two recessive 'orange' genes became orange.

This is obviously a very elementary look at genetics, but it might spark interest in your student to study the subject further. For more interesting topics and explanation, encourage your student to explore Gregor Mendel (the great Austrian botanist), Punnett squares, and other related subjects. Many books from your library will have interesting explanations of genes.

Language Arts:
Creative Writing—The Wittings One Year Later

Look with your student at the last page of our story, page 86—Anna's journal entry. She writes, "There will be flowers in the spring, and the river will run again. And in the spring there will be the new baby, Papa and Sarah's baby." Who does your student think the baby will look like? Will it be a boy or a girl? What will its name be? Will it rain enough to fill the cow pond for swimming?

Encourage your student to take these questions and more and write a short story of what life is like for the Wittings one year later. The baby would be a few months old and surely many things will have changed. What does your student think it will be like? This assignment can be as brief or lengthy as you deem appropriate. Remind your student to keep his characters consistent with how they have acted before. If the characters have changed, be sure to explain what happened that has caused their behavioral change. For instance, if Caleb becomes difficult or mean, perhaps he's jealous of the new baby or maybe no one is spending enough time with him, etc. Teach your student how to let his reader in on what's happening to his characters.

Issues of Human Relationships: Working Through Fears

Caleb is extremely frightened by the thought of staying in Maine. He wishes to go home to the prairie and he misses his father a great deal (pages 77, 79). He even wonders if Sarah has forgotten about going home. Has your student ever been afraid of a situation or person and tried to keep his feelings to himself? What happened? Was he able to work through them alone?

Sometimes when we are most frightened about something (an event or person) the best way to work through our fears is to share them with someone else. Trying to hold emotions inside can be tiring and stressful—and can make us even more afraid! Instead, talking with someone else can have many positive effects. Perhaps the other person is just as frightened as you are and can offer empathy and closeness (just like Anna did in the cove). Sometimes the other person, particularly if it's an older friend or relative, has experienced a situation like yours and can offer solutions and encouragement. Often, by talking to someone else, we come to realize new aspects of the problem we hadn't thought of before—reasons for us not to be afraid. Children sometimes think that only other children can understand what they are feeling—and sometimes that might be true. However, going to adults and parents can often be your best decision when you are nervous about something. They have experience and maturity which helps them understand what you are going through.

Encourage your student to be open with his fears and allow others to help him with his problems. It isn't 'cool' to be strong all the time. Sometimes we need to let people know what we're thinking and feeling. Knowing we can go to our friends and family with our concerns is one of our greatest comforts!

Writing and Discussion Question

Sarah is going to have a new baby. Take a moment and think about what you know of Sarah and Jacob's physical and emotional characteristics. What do they enjoy doing? What are they like? Now write a paragraph or page describing what you think the new baby will be like. Will he/she be plain like Sarah? Will he/she love the prairie like Papa? Will he/she be good with words, or will he/she speak between the lines? Be as creative as you can and bring in as many clues from the stories as you were able to find to help you.

Vocabulary Words

trait: a distinguishing characteristic

genetics: the branch of biology dealing with heredity

dominant: a gene which expresses itself most often

recessive: a gene which is only expressed occasionally

Internet Connections

To view current suggested links relating to this chapter's lessons, see www.fiveinarow.com/connections.

HELEN KELLER
BY MARGARET DAVIDSON

Chapter 1

Parent Summary

In chapter 1, we are introduced to Mr. and Mrs. Keller and their baby daughter, Helen. Helen was born as healthy as any other baby. When she was not yet two years old, she was stricken with scarlet fever. Helen was quite sick and nearly died. After a long while, her health began to improve, but her parents soon discovered the severe illness had left their daughter both blind and deaf.

What we will cover in this chapter:

History and Geography: The Time Frame of Our Story

History and Geography: Scarlet Fever—A Sickness of the Past

Science: Human Anatomy—The Eye

Language Arts: Mary Ingalls—Another Girl Blinded by Scarlet Fever

Fine Arts: Making Toys for Children—What You Must Consider

Lesson Activities

History and Geography: The Time Frame of Our Story

Draw you student's attention to page 8. Our author tells us that Helen was born almost 100 years ago. Look with your student at the year our book was written—1969. More than 30 years have passed since then. It has been over 115 years since Helen was born. Encourage your student to always balance any information he reads against the year the book was *written*. He will begin to notice points of view, vernacular and items mentioned that will give him clues for guessing the time frame of the story.

Our author doesn't tell us in the beginning of the book exactly what year Helen was born. However, if your student flips to page 92, he will see that she was born in 1880 and died in 1968. If you are keeping a journal or notebook for this unit, your student may wish to include a timeline of Keller's life, beginning in 1880. What other events were happening during that year or decade? (Examples: Vice President Chester A. Arthur becomes President of the United States after the assassination of President Garfield in 1881; by 1880 commercial food packers begin to use glass containers to package their products; the first electric streetcars and trains began to appear in America in the 1880s.)

History and Geography: Scarlet Fever—A Sickness of the Past

On page 8, we learn that Helen Keller was probably struck down with a disease called scarlet fever. Has your student ever heard of this illness? Scarlet fever is now extremely rare in the United States and Western Europe because doctors have used penicillin since the 1950s to treat the disease. It is called scarlet fever because of the trademark red rash which develops on the face and torso at the onset of the sickness.

Before the 1950s and particularly in the late 19th century, scarlet fever was a common and feared illness. With symptoms including sore throat, nausea, high fever and achy joints, scarlet fever often resulted in kidney infections, kidney dysfunction and blindness. Use this as an opportunity to explore the history of scarlet fever, or other aspects of infectious disease, epidemics, etc.

Science: Human Anatomy—The Eye

Helen is blind because of her illness (page 9). Her eyes no longer operate normally. But how do eyes really work, anyway? How do we see things? What are the different parts of an eye?

Take this wonderful opportunity to share with your student some information about the human eye.

Begin by drawing your student's attention to the main parts of the human eye. For example, the orbit (eye socket), pupil, iris, cornea, retina, tear ducts, eyelashes and lid. Each piece serves a specific and vital function for our sight. The human eyeball is about one inch in diameter, yet it can see and focus on objects smaller than the head of a pin, and as far away as the moon. Amazing, isn't it?

Explain to your student that our eye doesn't "see" objects in front of it. Instead, it absorbs light reflected off the objects and transmits that information to our brain. That is why we can't see anything in pitch-black darkness. In order for our eyes to function, some light must be present. As light rays enter our eye, the eye transforms these into electrical signals and sends them to the brain. The brain then interprets these signals as visual images.

More excellent topics for exploration in this unit might include diseases of the eye, such as glaucoma and cataracts. Why do some people need glasses while others don't? Nearsightedness is a common eye defect, and so is farsightedness. Does your student know that some people (almost exclusively men) cannot perceive colors properly? This is called color blindness. These individuals will confuse certain colors like greens and browns. This condition is not correctable; however, it does not worsen.

If your student is interested in learning more about the human eye, you may wish to spend more time exploring this topic together. By building a model of the eye, drawing pictures, dissecting a cow eyeball, getting books from the library and more, your student can gain a better understanding of this important section of their anatomy studies. If you are interested in doing a cow eye dissection, contact your local butcher or a slaughterhouse in your area. Eyes can be requested and held for you, usually at no charge. Try to arrange to pick up the eye on the day you plan to do the dissection. Fresh eyes are easier to dissect than old ones, because the connective tissues have not had a chance to solidify and toughen.

Enjoy exploring the world of vision and the human eye with your student. This is not only an interesting and fun section to study, but it is an important part of your student's science education.

Language Arts:
Mary Ingalls—Another Girl Blinded by Scarlet Fever

Many children have read and loved the classic series written by Laura Ingalls Wilder—*The Little House* series. If your student has not read these books, please encourage him to do so. Better yet, read them aloud together. Filled with fascinating historical information, family drama and beautiful character sketches, these books, while fiction, contain much of the true story of the life of Laura Ingalls Wilder.

If your student has already read and enjoyed these books, he may remember another little girl who was blinded by scarlet fever. Laura's sisters Mary, Carrie and Grace, along with Laura's mother, all contracted the illness, but only Mary was left without her sight. This sad event is located in the opening lines of *By the Shores of Silver Lake*—the fifth book in the series of nine. Here is an excerpt from that book:

The doctor had come every day; Pa did not know how he could pay the bill. Far worst of all, the fever had settled in Mary's eyes, and Mary was blind...Her blue eyes were still beautiful, but they did not know what was before them, and Mary herself could never look through them again, to tell Laura what she was thinking without saying a word...Pa had said she [Laura] must be eyes for Mary.

Enjoy making this literary connection with your student!

Fine Arts: Making Toys for Children—What You Must Consider

On page 10, Mrs. Keller uses one of Helen's toys to try to capture her daughter's attention. The toy is a can filled with stones. Does your student think this sounds like an enjoyable, or a boring toy? Certainly in our day and age, a rattle made from a can and rocks seems quite crude. But is it? What does your student think of the toys he sees for children today?

Today, we have highly sophisticated toys for children. Toys with lights, moving pieces, and even toys that interact with us. Sometimes, however, if you watch children and observe their playtime the most popular playthings are still the most simple, such as pots and pans, a large cardboard box or even an old-fashioned teddy bear.

Does your student have younger siblings or know a small child? Encourage him to design and make a toy for that child that is simple, safe and fun. What are things he should consider when designing his toy? The plaything should be safe, have visual appeal, be interesting and age appropriate for the child, be made of non-toxic materials, have no small pieces which could be swallowed and, most of all, should be something which brings delight. Your student may also consider various other factors in his design including shape, color, texture, etc.

There are all types of toys your student can think about—stuffed animals, pull toys, blocks and many more. Have fun inventing and creating an old-fashioned toy today!

Writing and Discussion Question

Why do you think Mrs. Keller screamed when she discovered Helen's blindness, and only whispered when she realized her daughter was also deaf? Discuss your ideas.

Internet Connections

To view current suggested links relating to this chapter's lessons, see www.fiveinarow.com/connections.

Chapter 2

Parent Summary

The doctor confirms Mr. and Mrs. Kellers' realizations—Helen is both deaf and blind. He tells them there is nothing they can do. They go for second and third opinions, only to hear the same response—no hope. As Helen grows, she develops her own 'language.' Certain gestures mean different things and her parents are able to slowly understand her a bit better—but not much. Most of the time, Helen is in a world of her own. As she grows older, she also grows more frustrated. Why can't she move her lips like other people? What are they doing? Why don't they understand her? The more frustrated Helen gets, the more aggressive and angry she becomes.

The Kellers soon have another baby girl, and this makes Helen even more out of control. Soon, the Kellers are out of ideas. They don't know what to do with Helen. Mrs. Keller reads an article about a school in Boston, the Perkins Institute. They once helped a little deaf and blind girl. As a last resort, Mr. Keller writes to Perkins, but without much hope of finding any answers.

What we will cover in this chapter:

History and Geography: Perkins Institute

Science: Sensory Deprivation Exercise

Science: 'Deaf and Dumb' Does *Not* Mean Ignorant

Issues of Human Relationships: Living with Hope and Determination

Lesson Activities

History and Geography: Perkins Institute

Mr. and Mrs. Keller write to Perkins Institute in Boston, hoping the school knows some way they can help Helen (page 19). Mrs. Keller has read an article about a little blind and deaf girl who had gone to that school before and she had learned to communicate with others. As background information, that little girl was the first student at Perkins who was both blind and deaf. She was the roommate of another little girl who also had vision problems—Anne Sullivan. Miss Sullivan is sent to teach Helen.

Today, Perkins is still in existence, helping the visually impaired and teaching parents and community classes on dealing with blindness. Under its new name, Perkins School for the Blind, people of all ages (birth to the elderly) can enroll in classes and receive training and information.

Your student can gather more specific information about Perkins School for the Blind at your local library.

You might also wish to locate Boston, Massachusetts on a map for your student. How far is Boston from Tuscumbia, Alabama?

Science: Sensory Deprivation Exercise

Helen is both blind and deaf. She can't hear any sound, no matter how loud, and she cannot see anything. Can you imagine being in such a dark and silent world? How would it feel? What would you have to rely on for information? How would it change the way you live your life every day? These are all questions you and your student can be thinking about throughout our study of the life of Helen Keller.

However, to gain a better understanding of how she felt, work with your student on some sensory deprivation exercises. Begin by explaining the exercise to your student. You will take him to an interior room of the house (e.g., bathroom, closet, basement). The darker the room is, the better the exercise will be. If you wish, mask off the cracks around a door jam or lay a towel at the base of the door to enhance the darkness. Now, place a blindfold over your student's eyes to complete the sight 'deprivation.' Next, your student will have cotton balls placed in his ears and stereo earphones or hearing protection head- phones or even earmuffs placed over that. The goal is to block out every sound your stu- dent might be able to detect.

Now, you and your student can both sit in the room for a pre-determined length of time (the longer your student is willing to sit, the better feel he will get for what it is like to be both blind and deaf). Anywhere from five minutes to fifteen minutes is a good amount of time.

Before the experiment takes place, however, have your student write down how he thinks it will feel to be 'blind and deaf.' Will it be much different? What will he have to rely on in order to gain information? Will he be comfortable or uncomfortable?

After the sensory deprivation experiment is complete, talk with your student about his experience. Was it exciting or frustrating? Did he get bored or was he scared? What could he 'feel' happening around him? Did he lose his concept of time? Did it seem much longer than he expected or shorter? Can he imagine living in a world like that all the time—like Helen? Does your student have a greater respect for Helen after the exper- iment?

Science: 'Deaf and Dumb' Does *Not* Mean Ignorant

Draw your student's attention to page 12. Our author tells us that Helen became "dumb." What does your student think this means? Explain to your student, if there is confusion, that in no way does dumb mean *ignorant* when used to describe deaf children. Instead, the word 'dumb' has been used in the past to denote someone who cannot speak. Because deaf children cannot hear others speaking, it is extremely difficult for them to imitate and learn speech. Imagine how hard it was for Helen, who could not hear or see others speaking! Even though Helen had already learned some words before she was sick with scarlet fever, after she became blind and deaf, she forgot all the words. Deaf children and blind children can be just as bright as any other children. Their disabilities do not in any way affect their intellect or abilities to learn and explore—as the life of Helen Keller certainly demonstrates.

Today, you rarely hear the words 'deaf and dumb' spoken together. The deaf com- munity has worked diligently to eradicate the word 'dumb' from the common vernacular because of the inferred meaning. Encourage your student to make friends with deaf and blind children. Even if he does not know sign language, deaf people are touched and excit- ed when people try to communicate with them. They will help you learn to speak their language.

Teach your student to appreciate everyone around him. *Everyone* has a great deal to offer each of us. No one should ever be called 'dumb.'

Issues of Human Relationships:
Living with Hope and Determination

Mr. and Mrs. Keller are very frustrated! Their little girl is becoming more and more of a struggle to raise and they don't know how to help her. Would you have thought of giving up? Most people probably would. But Mrs. Keller does not. She begs Helen's father to take one more chance and write to Perkins. Maybe there is someone who can help them with their daughter.

The Kellers are a wonderful example of determination. Being determined does not mean you are never discouraged. Instead, it means you don't allow that discouragement to bring you down and frustrate you. It means you have a sense of purpose and you work toward that goal.

Encourage your student today by sharing with him a struggle you have had where you felt like giving up. Did you? How were you able to work the problem out and live with hope and determination?

Writing and Discussion Questions

If you did the 'sensory deprivation' exercise, how did it feel? What was the strangest sensation? What did you miss the most? How does it help you to understand deaf and blind children better? Continue your essay, sharing other thoughts that you may have.

Internet Connections

To view current suggested links relating to this chapter's lessons, see www.fiveinarow.com/connections.

Chapter 3

Parent Summary

Mr. Keller's letter to Perkins Institute is soon answered. A teacher named Annie Sullivan is coming to help teach and instruct Helen. When she finally arrives one morning, Helen decides she doesn't like her. She has no idea Miss Sullivan has come to help her. Later on in the day, Helen gets into a fight with Miss Sullivan over a doll she has found. She ends up punching Annie in the face. Miss Sullivan knows the reason Helen is so misbehaving is that the Kellers have let her have her own way for so long. Annie is not sure how she can help change that, but she is going to have to try.

What we will cover in this chapter:

Science: Sound Is Vibration—An Experiment

Science: Exploring the Five Senses

Language Arts: Creative Writing—What Was Helen Thinking?

Fine Arts: A Movie Recommendation—*The Miracle Worker*

Lesson Activities

Science: Sound Is Vibration—An Experiment

On page 21 we see Helen 'listening' with her body, not her ears. Our author tells us Helen could feel the 'vibrations' coming through the air and ground. Are vibrations the same things as sounds? Take some time to discuss the scientific explanation of sound with your student.

Sounds are made by the vibrations of objects. When an object vibrates, it emits sound vibrations in all directions. When those waves hit our ears, our brain transfers them into sound. Sound travels through water, air and solid objects. Has your student ever read or heard about the Native American Indians putting their ears to the ground to hear the hoofbeats of horses in the distance? This practice works because solid ground transfers sound vibrations very well, and you can hear for a long distance.

Is your student still skeptical that sound is actually vibration? Here is a simple experiment to illustrate this principle. Locate a stereo speaker (or boom box turned on its back). Lay the speaker so the screen is face up. Have your student place a few grains of rice, lentils or small beans on the speaker. Now, select some music and start the volume out very softly. As the volume increases, the rice may begin to move a bit. As the volume gets quite loud, your student will be able to see the rice actually jump and quiver on top of the speaker. Why would this occur? Because sound is vibration! As the sound waves are produced by the stereo and the vibrations move out in all directions, they even hit the rice and move it.

Helen couldn't actually 'hear' the sounds like we can, but she certainly felt the sounds! Perhaps you've been to a commercial fireworks display and 'felt' the impact of large aerial bombs a second or two prior to 'hearing' them. Helen would have felt them, just like you or me, but would never have heard them a few moments later. If your student is interested in exploring this concept further, encourage him to locate more books at the library or an area bookstore. Other interesting related topics to explore are the Doppler Effect, sound interference, echoes and the human ear.

Science: Exploring the Five Senses

Ask your student how many senses humans have. What are the basic five? Taste, touch, hearing, sight and smell. Helen, unfortunately, does not have use of two of her senses—hearing and sight. What would it be like to live without one (or more) of your senses? How does your student think it would effect his life? How would he feel? Begin your exploration of this lesson by discussing with your student in brief how each of the basic five senses work. For example, taste is caused by cells on our tongue (taste buds or papillae) responding to molecules in the food or other substance, and transmitting information to the nerves and then to our brains.

Sight involves our eyes collecting light and transmitting the images to our brains. Has your student ever wondered why he can't see in the dark? That is because our ability to see is directly related to the light around us. Our eyes receive the light that is reflected off of images and objects. If there is no light, then our eyes think there is nothing there, even if our brain knows there is. For example, if your bedroom is extremely dark and you're walking through, you might bump into the bed. Your brain knows the bed is there, but if there isn't any light your eyes can't detect the object. If your student wishes to explore sight further, encourage him to learn more about the cornea, iris, light refraction, etc. Also, he may wish to go back and review the anatomy lesson on eyes located in chapter 1 of this unit.

Language Arts: Creative Writing—What Was Helen Thinking?

Reread pages 27 and 28 with your student. The author gives us a lot of details and information about what Miss Annie and Mrs. Keller are thinking and doing during the exchange with the doll. However, we are not completely sure of what Helen is thinking. Can you imagine? Suddenly some stranger is living in her home, giving her a 'gift' and then taking it away?

For a creative writing assignment, have your student write Helen's thoughts throughout this scenario. Who does Helen think Miss Annie is? Why is she there? When Miss Annie grabs the doll, what goes through the young girl's mind? Why does she decide to hit Miss Annie? When Helen runs away for the day, where does she go and what does she do? This creative writing exercise can be as long or short as you wish.

Fine Arts: A Movie Recommendation—*The Miracle Worker*

Excellent supporting material for this unit is the film *The Miracle Worker*. Made in 1962, this film adaptation of the play stars Patty Duke. It explores the story of Annie Sullivan and Helen Keller. The movie is superb and makes an excellent family film. If your student is younger, you may wish to preview it first, but be assured that it is a wonderful addition to this study of the life of Helen Keller. Be sure to look for added information not found in the story itself.

Writing and Discussion Question

On page 29, we read that Helen slept well that night, but Annie did not. Why do you think this was so? How do you think Mr. and Mrs. Keller slept? Why?

Internet Connections

To view current suggested links relating to this chapter's lessons, see www.fiveinarow.com/connections.

Chapter 4

Parent Summary

Helen continues to fight with Annie. The little girl can't understand why this stranger has come to her house! Helen gets angrier and Miss Annie doesn't quite know how to handle her. Every time she tries to discipline Helen or explain something, Mr. and Mrs. Keller jump into the conversation and Helen runs to them. After an entire day of battling with Helen over the breakfast table, Miss Annie is at her wit's end. She knows Helen needs to live away from home for awhile, but can she convince the Kellers?

What we will cover in this chapter:

Science: How Good Is Your Sense of Smell?

Language Arts: Writing Persuasive Argument

Lesson Activities

Science: How Good Is Your Sense of Smell?

Helen could tell where the last fat sausage was on the table. It was right on Miss Annie's plate (page 33)! Helen knew because she sniffed and smelled it out.

For a frivolous but fun activity, let your student try to 'sniff' out the last sausage. Prepare some sausages, perhaps for breakfast or brunch and let everyone join in the meal. When the eating is mostly finished, ask everyone to leave the room. Clear away all the sausages but one and leave it on one of the plates. Now, blindfold your student and invite him back into the eating area. No peeking!

Can your student find the one sausage that is left, just by using his sense of smell? What makes it difficult or easy to detect where the sausage is located? Do your students think that Helen's sense of smell might have been sharper than your own because of her disability?

Language Arts: Writing Persuasive Argument

Miss Annie has a new plan to help Helen, but she's not sure the Kellers will like it (page 38). She knows it will take the right words to convince them of her idea. The way in which Miss Annie will need to present her ideas is with persuasion. She will need to 'persuade' the Kellers that her idea is valid and workable. Has your student ever needed to persuade someone of something? Of course! Every day, we use persuasion in our conversation and our writing. For example, your student might ask a sibling, "Would you mind taking out the garbage even though it's my turn today? I'll be happy to do the dishes for you this evening." The first child is trying to 'persuade' the sibling to go along with his plan of swapping chores.

But is persuading someone always easy? No. Sometimes, it takes a lot of thought and pre-planning to present a logical persuasive argument. Take some time and share with your student a few tips on writing a persuasive paper.

When you write a persuasive argument, it is important that you pick a topic that is of extreme interest to *you*. If you are going to convince someone or change his mind on an issue, then *you* must believe in what you are saying. Persuasive paper topics are often issue debates. For example, your student might write a persuasive paper on: why hot lunches should be served in their school; why it's important to wear a bicycle helmet when you're riding; why the national film rating system should be changed by adding a rating between G and PG, etc.

As you prepare to write your paper, it is important that you investigate the topic. Ask other people their opinion. Why do they agree or disagree with your position? If they disagree with you, prompt conversations with them that will help you understand the opponent's side. This, in turn, will tell you what you will need to argue against in your paper. Be open and listen to all sides.

Next, do your research. Find articles, books, television reports and interviews where people discuss the topic you are covering. If it is a local or personal topic (for example, the hot lunch program), do interviews and ask a lot of questions.

Finally, begin to organize your findings. List the top three or four points you would like to make. Underneath each, list the supporting evidence and facts you have found.

Now you can begin writing your paper, following your outline and choosing your words carefully. When you are trying to persuade someone of your idea, it is never a good idea to offend or bully him. Instead, be logical. Present both sides of the issue and then explain, in concrete detail, why your position is better. Be positive. Don't put their ideas down, but instead show your audience how your ideas can work better for everyone. This is called being 'diplomatic.' Don't be overly emotional or irrational about your topic, but do let your audience know how you feel.

As you write, build strong images to support your idea. For example, "Every 15 minutes a child is taken to a hospital due to head injuries suffered from a bicycle accident." Encourage your audience by letting them know how agreeing with you will help them. What will they get out of it? How will their lives be changed? And save your most poignant arguments for the end of the paper or speech. Many of your listeners may withhold their decision until the very end—give them something to grab onto.

If your student is interested in trying to write a persuasive paper or speech, encourage him to pick a topic and give it a try. Then, after he has written or presented the completed assignment, be honest with him. How did you feel after reading or hearing it? Did he convince you? How could it have been better? What really worked?

Writing and Discussion Question

What do you think Miss Annie's idea is going to be? What is she planning to ask Mrs. Keller?

Internet Connections

To view current suggested links relating to this chapter's lessons, see www.fiveinarow.com/connections.

Chapters 5 and 6

Parent Summary

Miss Annie and Helen take up residence together in the Kellers' garden house. It was Miss Annie's idea to take Helen away from the family for awhile, and it works well. Each day, Helen learns more about Miss Annie, but she still doesn't understand what words are or what all of the 'finger' spelling in her hand means. Then one day the connection is made. Helen is playing in a fountain and as she feels the water Miss Annie spells 'water' into her hand. Helen understands! Helen understands that Miss Annie is her teacher and she learns her own name—*Helen*. Things are finally changing for Helen!

What we will cover in these chapters:

Language Arts: Etymology—The Study of Words

Language Arts: Creative Writing—The Smells of Spring

Issues of Human Relationships: Fostering Anticipation for Each New Day

Lesson Activities

Language Arts: Etymology—The Study of Words

Helen now understands that each item in the world has a name—a word that corresponds! We often take that concept for granted, but imagine making that discovery for the first time! Does your student know that there is a science, a study that is entirely devoted to the origins and development of words? It is called etymology [eht uh MAHL uh jee].

Share with your student that each word, just like a person, has its own country—its own history. Etymologists work diligently to uncover those facts and stories, as well as to identify changes in words even today. Languages change and go through modifications and additions constantly because societies change.

The earliest form of a word, in any given language, is called an etymon. Your student can think of etymons as mother words. For example, the word for father in Italian is 'padre', 'padre' in Spanish, 'pere' in French and 'pai' in Portuguese. What letter does your student think the etymon of these words begins with? The letter p. These words are alike because all these languages branch off of Latin. The Latin word for father is 'pater'—pater is the etymon.

Sometimes etymologists work on finding the origins of combination words. For example, the word smog is a combination of the words smoke and fog. What about funny words like 'scribble?' That word comes from the Latin word meaning *to write*—scribere.

And what about the word 'etymology?' How did we come up with that word? Like many words, it helps make the word easier to understand to break it into pieces. Words often have a prefix and/or a suffix. The suffix 'ology' in the word 'etymology' means 'the study of.' And the prefix 'etym' is Latin for 'word.' Etymology then means 'the study of words.' Pursue this fascinating field by doing additional study. You might begin with a dictionary. Look for books on etymology or do an introductory overview of Latin. Learning about our words can be fascinating.

Language Arts: Creative Writing—The Smells of Spring

Draw your student's attention to page 41. We read, "The window was open and the smells of spring came pouring in." What does your student think the author means by the 'smells of spring?' What does spring smell like?

For a creative writing assignment, ask your student to make a list of the smells he associates with springtime. He might record smells such as flowers, even particular ones such as daffodils, hyacinths, lilacs, etc., rain and fresh-cut grass. For your older student, make this exercise even more challenging by talking through specific descriptions of each item. For example, how would he describe the smell of fresh-cut grass? Make a list of the descriptive words for each item:

Newly Cut Grass

Pungent
Acidic
Lemony
Fresh

If your student is doing this lesson during the summer, fall or winter, encourage him to use his sensory memory. If he can think back to a spring day, he can remember the smells and describe them. Happy spring!

Issues of Human Relationships: Fostering Anticipation for Each New Day

On page 44 we read that the day Helen begins to understand words and the world, April 5th, 1887, began like any other day. Neither Teacher nor Helen knew what an important day it would be. Encourage your student to approach each new day as though something wonderful could happen. By fostering anticipation each morning, we lead more excited, positive lives. Talk with your student about the difference between optimism and pessimism and how those outlooks color both our emotions and our experience.

Writing and Discussion Question

When Helen figures out that everything has a name, Miss Annie begins to laugh and sob (page 44). Can someone laugh and sob at the same time? Why would those two different emotions go together? Explain.

Imagine trying to describe subjective feelings to someone who has never known the words—someone like Helen. How would you describe sadness? Love? Joy? Discuss.

Vocabulary Words

etymology: the study of words

etymon: the original, root word

To view current suggested links relating to this chapter's lessons, see www.fiveinarow.com/connections.

Chapter 7

Parent Summary

Teacher makes sure that Helen has all the same experiences that any child would. Helen gets to go to the zoo, attend the circus, bake Christmas cookies and enjoy a canary for a pet. Helen is doing very well. Soon, she begins to learn to read Braille—the raised symbol language of the blind. In just one year, Helen has learned so much! Teacher knows it's time to learn even more.

What we will cover in this chapter:

History and Geography: The Circus

History and Geography: Louis Braille

Science: Primates

Language Arts: Creative Writing—Frosty Fingertips

Fine Arts: Juggling

Lesson Activities

History and Geography: The Circus

Helen enjoys the circus very much! There are so many new and exciting things for her to smell and touch at the circus—the clowns, the animals and much more (page 57). Has your student ever been to a circus before? Perhaps the largest and most famous touring circus in America (and abroad) is The Ringling Bros. and Barnum & Bailey Three Ring Circus. There are, however, many local and regional circus groups who provide delightful and entertaining shows right near your home.

What are the things your student thinks of when he thinks of a circus? What comes to mind first? Probably clowns. But what else? There are animals, a man on stilts, a band playing music, trapeze artists, juggling acts, cotton candy, popcorn, and of course, the ringmaster!

Who first thought of the idea for a 'circus?' Where do circuses come from? To answer these questions, first look at the word 'circus.' Circus comes from the Latin word for circle or oval shape. For more years than we are sure about (at least 2,000), circus-type shows have been presented in rings or oval shaped areas. Today, most circuses are held in large arenas or tents, but the acts are still framed within a ring or rings. Has your student ever heard of a 'three-ring circus?'

Although for many years circus groups traveled by train from town to town, today most move their acts, animals and people by truck. The Ringling Bros. and Barnum & Bailey is the only circus which still travels by railroad. Because the circus travels for months at a time, larger circus groups may have their own doctor, vet, barber and even school for the young performers.

The people who help set up the circus are known as roustabouts. The performers in any given act are most often married or related. That is how many tricks and acts are taught—children learn it from their parents. For example, you might see an act of liberty horses (horses without riders, doing patterns and tricks) being led by a couple. They might be the third generation of liberty horse trainers.

If your student is interested in learning more about circuses, here are some topic ideas for exploration: train travel and the circus; P.T. Barnum; Circus World Museum in Baraboo, Wisconsin; Lillian Leitzel (aerial performer from the 1930s); Gunther Gebel-Williams (famous wild animal trainer); and the famous circus clown, Emmett Kelly.

History and Geography: Louis Braille

Your student has probably already noticed, but draw his attention to the back cover of our book—*Helen Keller*. Let him feel the raised dot alphabet. Can he close his eyes and detect the differences between the letters? Does he think reading Braille would be easy or difficult? Share with your student some of the fascinating facts regarding the developer of this language—Louis Braille.

Born on January 4, 1809, Louis Braille was much like Helen Keller when she was born—a healthy, seeing, hearing child. It was not until he was three years old that Louis had an accident and became blind. At first, his eyes were just blurry. Before he reached the age of four, Louis became completely blind. Luckily, his parents had a place to turn. In 1819, when Louis Braille was ten years old, he was sent to a special school for the blind—the Royal Institute for Blind Youth in Paris, France. Founded in 1784, this school was the first of its kind. In those days, blind children were left to fend for themselves. Unable to go to regular schools, they never learned to read or write and were often left to beg for money. Not Louis. At the Royal Institute he made friends with other blind children and learned to read, write and do arithmetic.

But Louis was frustrated. The only way for blind people to read books was to follow along with their finger on the pages of embossed books. These books were expensive, heavy and very large. Each letter of each word had to be raised and widely spaced so the students could tell what letter it was. Reading was a slow process and writing was even slower. There had to be an easier way!

When Louis Braille was only 13 years old, he began working on a new system of writing—a code system based on the secret military codes of the French Army. Slowly but surely, Braille worked out the 26-letter alphabet by using raised dots in a 6-dot cluster. Each dot was numbered, and by punching the dots into paper in various combinations, could be felt on the opposite side. Each dot pattern represented a different letter of the alphabet. By the tender age of 15, Louis Braille had developed an entirely new language! Using nothing more than the 6-dot cell, Louis worked out 63 characters—the alphabet, numbers, punctuation symbols and commonly used words.

To write in this new raised-dot system, Braille also developed a special writing tool—a stylus. The paper slipped into a metal frame, and a metal pen (stylus) slid along the paper and was guided by a ruler. The writer could punch holes in the paper and then slide the ruler down to start on the next line. When the paper was flipped over, another person could 'read' the writing with his fingers.

Braille was a success! His system made books for the blind affordable, since the dots were easy to reproduce and took up little more space than conventional printed text. The letters and symbols were easy to learn! Imagine developing such an important invention before reaching the age of 16!

By age 20, Louis Braille became a teacher at the Royal Institute. Throughout his remaining years, Braille continued to work diligently as a teacher and advocate for the blind. Although his health began failing at a young age, Braille continued to support his students and friends. He died on January 6, 1852, just two days after his 43rd birthday.

Today, Louis Braille rests in the Pantheon in Paris—the burial place of France's most famous heroes. The house he grew up in, in Coupvray, France, has been preserved as a museum and looks much as it did when little Louis was growing up there. A plaque on the front door reads:

In this house on January 4, 1809, was born Louis Braille, the inventor of the system of writing in raised dots for use by the blind. He opened the doors of knowledge to all those who cannot see.

If your student is interested in learning more about this fascinating inventor and hero, the author strongly encourages you to locate the book by Russell Freedman, entitled *Out of Darkness—The Story of Louis Braille*. Written in lyrical prose, this book is powerful and compelling for adults as well as children. The illustrations by Kate Kiesler are beautiful, too. This book is truly wonderful for an outside resource in this unit! It cannot be recommended highly enough. Find it today!

Remind your student that like Louis Braille, he is never too young to have a good idea and help change the world!

Science: Primates

Helen is lucky enough to get to play with the monkeys at the circus (page 59)! Wouldn't that be fun? If your student has not yet had an opportunity to study monkeys, apes and primates, seize this learning opportunity and spend some time exploring them together. Does your student know that monkeys and apes (gorillas, chimpanzees, or orangutans) are not the same thing? Many people use the terms interchangeably. Look at pictures of each. Apes are generally considered smarter than monkeys and don't have tails! Apes are also wonderful climbers, while monkeys usually run and jump into the trees.

Monkeys include marmosets, tamarins, capuchins and baboons. When monkeys walk, they usually do so on all fours. Many monkeys can walk upright and even run on two legs, but only for a short time. Baboons groom one another for social activity. Most baboons spend several hours a day either being groomed or grooming another monkey. They seem to bond and enjoy this activity very much.

If your student is interested in learning more about primates, topics to explore might include: how monkeys communicate; the two main types of primates (1) anthropoids—humans and apes, (2) prosimians—lemurs and galagos; the predators of apes and monkeys; how they care for their young, etc. Find a good chart of the Animal Kingdom and see where the primates are located.

Language Arts: Creative Writing—Frosty Fingertips

Helen tells Teacher that some people have "frosty fingertips" while others have hands that "warm my heart." Do you suppose Helen was talking about the character of the person by using the metaphor of fingers and hands? Does your student know a person who is kind and good? A person who warms their heart? And does your student know people who are harder to get along with—quick to argue or take offense? Perhaps Helen would describe this second group as 'frosty.'

To continue this line of thought, have your student write a creative assignment, describing a person who has 'frosty fingertips.' What does the person look like? What is he/she wearing? What does the person do for a living? How do they talk to others? Encourage your student to include as many details as he can in the description and narrative. The reader should be able to picture just what the author was thinking.

Fine Arts: Juggling

Helen loved the circus. What is more traditional to the circus than clowns juggling? Anyone can learn to juggle. Circus camps and clown schools offer classes in the sport. Many bookstores, toy stores or gift shops sell beginning juggling sets. Juggling isn't a modern pastime only. Ancient paintings in Egyptian tombs show people juggling objects. For hundreds of years, court jesters performed juggling acts for kings and queens. Juggling is taken quite seriously by thousands of performers today. There is even an association just for them! The International Jugglers Association was formed in 1947. Juggling provides entertainment, both for the juggler and the person watching. For the juggler, it also develops excellent hand and eye coordination and provides exercise.

With a trio of beanbags or balls and a book explaining the basics, your student can learn this art as well! To make it easier for a beginner, encourage your student to practice standing by the edge of a bed. In this way, when he drops a ball (and everyone drops many when they're learning!), he can quickly pick it up without bending all the way to the ground. He will also find it easier to juggle with a plain, light-colored wall in the background to lessen visual distractions.

Your student can have a wonderful time learning an art as ancient as kings. Juggling is a marvelous vehicle for improving eye-hand coordination and for a surprising number of individuals, juggling becomes a lifelong hobby. Many enjoy learning to juggle with a partner, exchanging clubs and batons. Have fun exploring this fascinating activity.

Writing and Discussion Question

On page 64, Teacher decides it is time for Helen to move on. Do you think Helen is ready to go to school with other children? Has she learned enough yet? How would other children relate to her? How would you relate to her? Explain.

Vocabulary Words

Braille: the special coded raised-dot language of the blind

Louis Braille: the inventor of the language of the blind

primate: any of the highest ranking order of mammals (including humans, monkeys and apes)

Internet Connections

To view current suggested links relating to this chapter's lessons, see www.fiveinarow.com/connections.

Chapter 8

Parent Summary

Teacher enrolls Helen in the Perkins Institute—the same school Teacher went to when she was a girl. The same school that Mr. Keller wrote to when he asked for help for Helen. The teachers and students at Perkins love Helen. Helen loves her classes and the books she's given to read. Helen never knew how much there was available to her. When there are books that are not in Braille, Helen asks Teacher to read them to her.

Helen is nine years old now, and she spells so fast with her fingers people have to ask her to slow down. Her brain is faster than her fingers. Helen decides on a way to remedy this. She will learn to talk like a hearing child. At first, Teacher is hesitant, but she finally agrees. Helen works tireless hours trying to get her vocal cords to make the same vibrations she feels other people's throats making. Finally she says her first sentence: "I am not dumb now."

What we will cover in this chapter:

History and Geography: Robert Fulton—Steamboats

History and Geography: Plymouth Rock

History and Geography: Anne Sullivan's Life—Teacher

Career Path: Speech Therapist

Lesson Activities

History and Geography: Robert Fulton—Steamboats

On page 66, we see Helen taking her first steamboat ride. Remember, the year was around 1889. Steamboats had been cruising the waters of the world for nearly 70 years. But who invented the first steamboat? Share with your student some introductory information about this famous invention and the man behind it.

Born in 1765, Robert Fulton lived in Pennsylvania. His father was a farmer, but the young Robert showed more of a penchant for inventing. He made his own lead pencils and designed the fireworks for his town's annual celebration. Before the age of 16, Fulton had designed and built his own rifle, complete with sight and bore of original design.

When he was 21 years old Fulton moved to England to study art, but soon became more enamored with scientific developments. He loved to design new canal plans and explored the use of canal locks. In 1797, Fulton decided to concentrate on designing submarines. He built a diving boat called the *Nautilus* that could descend 24 feet in the water. But Fulton was still looking at new ideas.

In 1802, Fulton began to devote all of his attention to building a steam propulsion boat. In just one year, he set his first steamboat on the water, but it sunk. The engine was too heavy. Not to be dissuaded, Fulton kept working on his concept. On August 17, 1807, the first successful steamboat, the *Clermont*, set sail. A statue of Fulton resides in Washington, D.C., in honor of this great inventor.

[**Teacher's Note**: An excellent book to get for your student if he is interested in inventions is Steven Caney's *Invention Book*. As the cover says, "From inspiration to prototype, everything you need to know. Featuring easy at-home projects to start now, plus 35 Great American Invention Stories." This book is so enjoyable to look through. It explores the inventions of things from the zipper to chocolate chip cookies. This book could become a family favorite!]

If your student is interested in learning more about this topic, he might explore ship building, ship yards, canals and locks, the War of 1812 and Robert Fulton in greater detail.

History and Geography: Plymouth Rock

Teacher lets Helen stand on Plymouth Rock! If your student has not already studied the Pilgrims and their landing, take this learning opportunity to explore this event together.

According to popular stories, when the Pilgrim explorers aboard the *Mayflower* first set foot on American soil, they stepped on a giant granite boulder. More probably, the large boulder was simply visible and near the place where the Pilgrims came ashore. They christened the stone Plymouth Rock, in honor of their arrival. The rock was moved several times until 1921, when it was finally set permanently by the shore as a tribute to the Pilgrims and their landing in 1620.

If you are lucky enough to live near this site, by all means plan a field trip today!

History and Geography: Anne Sullivan's Life—Teacher

On page 68, we see Teacher and Helen reading a story together. Teacher is forced to stop because her eyes get too weak and tired. Why is that? Although our book goes into the reason briefly, take a few moments and share with your student some additional information on the life of Helen Keller's teacher—Anne Mansfield Sullivan.

Born in 1866 in Massachusetts, the young Anne Sullivan had vision problems. In just a short period of time, Anne became almost completely blind, becoming a student at the Perkins Institution for the Blind. Interesting to note, Miss Sullivan's roommate for a time was the first blind-deaf child ever educated in the United States—Laura Bridgman. By being around Laura, Anne gained understanding and compassion for those stricken with both deafness and blindness. In 1881 and again in 1887, Anne Sullivan had corrective surgeries done on her eyes that were quite successful. But, although her vision was restored, her eyes would always be weak. Anne Sullivan wore dark glasses most of her life. Toward her later years, her eyes began to worsen again.

Anne Sullivan devoted her entire life to helping Helen Keller. Sullivan married, at age 38, a Harvard professor named John A. Macy. Even after the marriage, she continued to travel with Miss Keller. Anne Sullivan died on October 19, 1936. Helen Keller and Teacher had been together for 50 years.

If your student is interested in learning more about the life of Anne Sullivan, the Scholastic Biography series you're using now also has published a biography on the life of Miss Sullivan. Entitled *Helen Keller's Teacher*, it is available in most major bookstores and libraries. You may also want to branch out to study others who have spent a lifetime serving others.

Career Path: Speech Therapist

Helen is trying to learn to speak. At first, your student may not comprehend how difficult this would be for a person who is both blind and deaf. When we are children, we learn to speak by both hearing our parents and others and by observing the shape of their mouths and lips. Deaf children can learn to speak a little sometimes, by watching people. Blind children don't have much trouble at all because they can hear and imitate. But what if you could do neither?

Many people, not just those who are deaf, have trouble speaking. Sometimes people lisp, or stutter or can't pronounce certain letters or phrases. Often these problems plague people all their lives, but sometimes they are caused by a traumatic injury—stroke, brain injury or emotionally devastating event. How can people like these be helped? People called speech therapists work diligently with victims of speech impediments and help them learn to speak clearly and gain confidence.

If your student is interested in speech and how it works, and enjoys serving others and helping people overcome problems, a career in speech therapy might be a wonderful job to explore.

Speech therapists work in schools, deaf education centers, hospitals, nursing homes, private practices and public clinics. Students can earn a bachelor's degree and a master's degree in speech pathology/therapy.

The classes you might take in a college program for speech pathology/therapy include phonetics of American English, language development, language disorders in children, audiology, and the neuro-anatomical (brain) functions of speech.

If your student is interested in learning more about speech therapy, contact your local hospital or school. Arrange a visit to a learning center for children or speech pathology office. You may be able to have your student "shadow" a professional for the day, or simply observe him in a classroom setting.

Writing and Discussion Question

Some people in the deaf community do not think deaf children should try to speak. They believe that deaf children are special the way they are and shouldn't try to communicate like hearing children. What do you think about this? Do you agree with Helen's attempt at learning to speak? Why or why not?

Internet Connections

To view current suggested links relating to this chapter's lessons, see www.fiveinarow.com/connections.

Chapter 9

Parent Summary

Helen becomes more and more independent. She learns to ride a horse, swim by herself and even rides a tandem bicycle with a friend. Soon, Helen decides she wants to go to college. She and Teacher head off to Radcliffe College for women. Helen is forced to work twice as hard as the other girls. Teacher works hard, too. Both women go to class each day and Helen memorizes all she can. She reads so many Braille books her fingertips bleed. But in the fall of 1904, Helen graduates from Radcliffe with honors! She is the best educated deaf-blind person in the world!

What we will cover in this chapter:

History and Geography: 1892 President—Benjamin Harrison

History and Geography: Harvard University and Radcliffe College

Language Arts: Book Recommendation—*Black Beauty*

Fine Arts: Cooking—Helen Keller's Roasted Apples

Lesson Activities

History and Geography: 1892 President—Benjamin Harrison

On page 74, we read that 12-year-old Helen is invited to the White House to meet the President of the United States. Who would that have been? If you wish, you might have your student figure out which president it is himself. Helen was born in 1880. If she were 12, then the year would be 1892. Who was president through 1892? By looking in an encyclopedia or other reference book, your student should be able to discover that it was Benjamin Harrison. Here is a great opportunity to explore together with your student some of the history behind this president and a few interesting facts about his life. If you are keeping any kind of timeline or notebook for these units, make an entry for this American leader.

Benjamin Harrison was born in Ohio on August 20, 1833. His father was a congressman and farmer, and his mother was a housewife and mother of thirteen children. Because of his father's political life, Benjamin grew up in the public arena. Even more crucial to his decision to run for President, perhaps, was his grandfather, William Henry Harrison. William was the first Harrison to become President of the United States (9th President). Sadly, however, President William Harrison caught a severe cold on the day he gave his inaugural speech and died in office just one month later. His grandson, Benjamin had aspirations to be President from an early age, and in fact, ran under the slogan and song, "Grandfather's Hat Fits Ben."

Benjamin Harrison served as the commander and chief of a regiment of volunteers in the Civil War and moved through the ranks to become a brigadier general. His soldiers were quite fond of him, and affectionately called him "Little Ben" because he was not quite 5'6" tall.

Benjamin Harrison ran in the presidential elections of 1888 and beat incumbent, President Grover Cleveland. While in the White House, Harrison worked diligently to strengthen the country. His largest accomplishment was establishing more respect and honor for the flag of the United States. It was President Benjamin Harrison who insisted the flag fly over the White House government buildings and all schools. When you see a flag flying, think of President Benjamin Harrison.

Although he served a productive term, during the elections of 1892 he was defeated by his old rival, Grover Cleveland (who then served a second (but not sequential), presidency from 1893-1897). Sadly, just two weeks before this loss at the polls, Benjamin's wife, Caroline, died. He and his daughter were devastated.

After his presidency, Harrison returned to Ohio and practiced law. He married the nurse who took care of his wife during her last days, and had a daughter with her. He authored a book, traveled extensively and died in his home on March 13, 1901.

If your student is interested in learning more about Benjamin Harrison, encourage him to research the president at your library or on-line. If your student enjoys musicals, there is a delightful Disney film entitled *Family Band* featuring Buddy Ebsen, Richard Crenna, and Leslie Ann Warren. The film centers around a musical family that is politically divided. Most of the family feels allegiance to Benjamin Harrison but the grandfather supports Grover Cleveland. The climax of the film centers around the elections. This movie would make an entertaining addition to your study of our 23rd president—Benjamin Harrison!

History and Geography: Harvard University and Radcliffe College

Helen wanted to go to Harvard University (page 78). Teacher didn't think Helen could do the work in college, but she used the excuse, "Not Harvard, Helen. That's a boy's school." Later, Helen goes to Radcliffe College. Take this opportunity, if there is interest, and share with your student some information about these famous universities.

Harvard University is the oldest institution of higher learning in the United States of America—established in 1636 under the name 'Newtowne.' The school was renamed for John Harvard, a Puritan minister, who left the campus half of his estate and over 400 books when he died in 1638. Harvard has maintained a fierce pride and remains one of the top universities in the U.S. today. In fact, the school still operates under a charter written in 1650. With an endowment (money given to a school to maintain costs) of over $4 billion, Harvard is also one of the richest and most prestigious colleges in the country. Some of Harvard's most famous alumni include: Presidents John Adams, John Quincy Adams, Theodore Roosevelt, Franklin D. Roosevelt, John F. Kennedy and George W. Bush.

Radcliffe College was established in 1879 as the 'Harvard Annex.' It was, in all respects, a sister campus which provided instruction for women at the level they would have received at Harvard. In 1894 it was renamed, Radcliffe College.

The college Helen went to, Radcliffe, today is joined with Harvard as a 'sister' college. The two universities have joined admissions, but men are admitted to Harvard and women to Radcliffe. Although all classes are co-educational, every student (male or female) receives a degree from Harvard University. Radcliffe College is an independent institution legally and fiscally, but is in all other respects connected to Harvard.

Language Arts: Book Recommendation—*Black Beauty*

Helen's horse was named Black Beauty. Helen may or may not have named her horse after the famous Anna Sewell novel. Nonetheless, this is an excellent opportunity to make reference to the classic book. If your student has not already read or heard the wonderful tale of a horse and his masters, then take this time and introduce him to the book.

Written by Anna Sewell in 1877, *Black Beauty* is the fictional autobiography of a horse and his different masters. Because the book is written from the point of view of Black Beauty, your student will gain insight into writing from different perspectives. The book is also a moral tale about the treatment of animals and how we should all strive to be good and loving masters.

Sewell was born in England in 1820 and only lived to be 58 years old. When she was 14 she suffered a severe sprain to both ankles and remained crippled for the rest of her life. Her favorite times, both as child and adult, were when she was on her horse or in her horse-drawn carriage. She wrote *Black Beauty* over the course of six years while she was confined to her bed with an illness. It was her only book, but gained international renown. Today she is considered to be one of the most beloved childhood writers and her only book is still extremely popular.

The story is masterfully written and lovingly told. Find it, and begin a read-aloud time with your student today!

Fine Arts: Cooking—Helen Keller's Roasted Apples

Helen loved adventure and new experiences, but she also enjoyed quiet evenings at home. Our book tells us that sometimes she and Teacher made roasted apples and played games in front of the fire. Why not take a break and let your student cook up something special? Here is a recipe for roasted apples the way Helen might have fixed them herself:

Helen Keller's Roasted Apples

4 apples, peeled whole and cored
4 Tbs. butter or margarine
8 Tbs. brown sugar
4 Tbs. raisins
1/4 cup water

Preheat oven to 375° F. Set the 4 cored apples in a shallow glass or ceramic baking dish. Place 1 Tbs. butter, 2 Tbs. brown sugar, and 1 Tbs. raisins in the core of each apple. Then pour the water into the dish and bake, covered, for 35-45 minutes or until the apples are soft. Enjoy!

Writing and Discussion Question

Why do you think Anne Sullivan was so extremely devoted to Helen? Explain.

Vocabulary Word

tandem: made for two; two people working together; a bike for two; a pair

Internet Connections

To view current suggested links relating to this chapter's lessons, see www.fiveinarow.com/connections.

Chapter 10

Parent Summary

After graduating from Radcliffe, Helen begins to do all she can to help other blind and deaf people. She writes papers and then gives speeches. These provide forums where people can ask her questions and she can speak on the issues closest to her heart. On October 19, 1936, Helen suffers her greatest loss. Annie Sullivan dies. Helen finds the times very difficult, but she bravely continues. World War II has begun, and she travels to hospitals in the United States, encouraging the wounded and telling her story. Helen's life is never without adventure. She lives to be 87 years old, and dies on June 1, 1968. She continues to be an inspiration and hero to millions even today.

What we will cover in this chapter:

[Teacher's Note: The main lesson opportunity in this chapter is an exploration of World War II. If you have not already done so, put heavy emphasis on this important historical event. Investigate and explore the various topics given below and encourage your student to put together a notebook or poster set of his WWII studies. This major event in American history deserves a thorough study.]

Lesson Activities

History and Geography:
World War II—A Brief Overview and Ideas for Exploration

Helen Keller spent a great deal of time visiting WWII veterans in hospitals around the United States. She had compassion, particularly for those who were blinded during battle. Franklin D. Roosevelt asked her if she would be willing to help show the soldiers that life was still worth living (page 87).

Here is an excellent learning opportunity for your student—a beginner's look at World War II. Although there is no way to give a 'brief' look at such a major historical event, this lesson will be an attempt to examine some of the more important points. Specifically, this lesson will try to present to you a variety of ideas for your student to explore. Find an interest and then pursue that interest through the lens of World War II.

To begin, World War II is considered by nearly every expert to have been the most devastating war of all time. It killed more people, destroyed more property and infrastructure, and had more far-reaching consequences than any war before that time or after. The number of casualties due to the war will never be completely calculated, but according to several sources they are estimated to be over 17 million. Nearly 8 million soldiers from the Soviet Union alone! More than 19 million Soviet Union civilians were killed as a direct result of the fighting and bombing.

World War II began on September 1, 1939, when the Germans invaded Poland. Germany's dictator, Adolf Hitler, had been working systematically to make Germany into the most feared and powerful nation in the world. He had, in many ways, succeeded. In only ten months, his armies soundly defeated and conquered Poland, Denmark, Luxembourg, the Netherlands, Belgium, Norway and France! Great Britain stood alone, but strong, against Hitler. Then, forces began to join Germany—Italy and Japan. These three countries formed one side of the war—they became known as the Axis. Together they invaded northern Africa and the Soviet Union.

Japan attacked the United States military base at Pearl Harbor, Hawaii on December 7, 1941. This brought the United States into the war full force, and they soon formed their own alliance. The United States, Great Britain, China and the Soviet Union formed what they called the Allies. By the end of the war, nearly 50 countries would be a part of the Allies.

The bloody battles continued throughout 1944. In the background of all the fighting, the Allies had a 'trump' card, however. In 1939, the scientist Albert Einstein had informed President Roosevelt that he believed he could build a 'super bomb'—a nuclear bomb which would be unparalleled in its intensity because the explosion would occur from the splitting of an atom. Einstein was afraid Germany would develop the bomb before the United States. Interestingly enough, Einstein had been born in Germany. Immediately, the President ordered testing to begin and the 'Manhattan Project' was birthed.

On May 7, 1944, Germany, finally broken and penniless, surrendered to the Allies. President Roosevelt died in April of 1945, while the war was still being fought. Harry S. Truman became President. He, along with many Americans, was sickened by the length and devastation of WWII. He wanted the fighting to stop. He, along with Great Britain and China, sent Japan an ultimatum. If they did not surrender, American forces would destroy Japan. Japan refused to back down.

As a result, on August 6, 1945, a large American bomber (the *Enola Gay*) dropped the first atomic bomb ever used in battle on the Japanese city of Hiroshima. The blast killed approximately 100,000 people instantly and completely leveled nearly five square miles of land. Still, the Japanese did not surrender. So, the President ordered a second bomb to be dropped on Nagasaki, just three days later. Japan's Emperor Hirohito pleaded with the government to surrender. On September 2, 1945, Japan formally ended the war. That day, as named by Truman, is still known as V-J Day, or Victory over Japan Day. World War II had finally ended.

From this catastrophic event in our history, the United Nations (UN) was founded. The war had been so horrifying and devastating, that no one wanted a tragedy like that to occur ever again. In October of 1945, a new charter went into effect, signed by delegates from 50 different countries. The United Nations works tirelessly today to prevent conflicts and to help nations maintain peaceful relations.

There are innumerable linked topics for your student to explore when looking at World War II. What were some of the causes of the war? (World War I, The Treaty of Versailles, nationalism, the rise of dictatorships) What were some of the consequences? (casualties, buildings and land destruction, displaced persons) What ships were used? Submarines? Airplanes? The Atomic Bomb. Also, Presidents Roosevelt and Truman. Albert Einstein. The Manhattan

Project. Adolf Hitler. Pearl Harbor. The U.S. home-front (the effects on family life, women's issues and the work force). The entertainers and celebrities who traveled to encourage the troops (Bob Hope, Bing Crosby, Dinah Shore, and more).

For further connections, here are some other things that were happening during the years of WWII.

1939: The movie, *The Wizard of Oz* (Judy Garland) came out. Popular songs were: "God Bless America," "Over the Rainbow," and "I'll Never Smile Again."

1940: Ernest Hemingway wrote, *For Whom the Bell Tolls*. Duke Ellington became a popular composer and jazz musician. The population of the United States reached 132 million.

1941: The Panama Canal construction began. New York won the World Series from Brooklyn (4-1). Great Britain began to encourage 'clothing rationing' because of the cloth shortage due to WWII.

1942: The Disney film *Bambi* was released. Enrico Fermi (U.S. scientist with the Manhattan Project) successfully splits the atom. The first automatic computer is developed in the United States.

1943: The movie *Casablanca* won an Academy Award. The Rodgers and Hammerstein musical play *Oklahoma* reached over 2,248 performances. George Washington Carver, U.S. scientist, died on January 5.

1944: The Ringling Bros. and Barnum & Bailey had a fire in Hartford, which killed more than 165 people.

1945: President Truman takes over in office. The Empire State Building was struck by a B-25 bomber on the 78-79 floors on July 28.

Have a fun and educational "voyage" with your student as you begin to explore World War II and the times that surrounded it.

Writing and Discussion Question

Helen said many times, "The best and most beautiful things in the world cannot be seen or even touched. They must be felt with the heart." What did Helen mean by this? In your opinion, what are some things, which can only be felt with the heart?

Internet Connections

To view current suggested links relating to this chapter's lessons, see www.fiveinarow.com/connections.

Master Index

Scope of Topics for *Beyond Five in a Row* Volume 2

Sarah, Plain and Tall

History and Geography
Maine and Eastern United States
Life in ME 'Down Easterners'
North Atlantic Seacoast
Life on the Rocky Coast
Flora
Fauna
Prairie
Life on the Flora
Fauna
Regions in America
Central Texas
South Dakota
North Dakota
Iowa
Illinois
Kansas
Nebraska
Oklahoma

Science
Biology
Animals of the sea
Whales
Orca
Sperm
Beluga
Killer
Dolphin
Porpoise
Seals
Ringed
So. Elephant
Crabeater
Blubber
Animals with shells
Mussels
Clams
Scallops
Shells
Made of calcium carbonate
Univalve
Bivalve
Birds of Prey
Marsh Hawk
Sharp-shinned hawk
Broad-winged hawk
Red-shouldered hawk
Galapagos hawk
Sparrow hawk
Falconry
Eagles, Buzzards
Vultures
Sand dunes
Traverse dunes
Barchan duns
Seif dunes
Star dunes
Mature sand

Water resources
Squalls

Language Arts
Continuing symbolism
Learning to infer
Alliteration
Character development
The Newbery Medal
ALSC (Association of Library Service to Children
Hyperbole
How to end a story

Literature explored:
Alice's Adventures in Wonderland by Lewis Carroll

Vocabulary Words
gestation
igneous
metamorphic
sedimentary
symbol
R.S.V.P.
cliché
advection fog
frontal fog
upslope fog
radiation fog
holding capacity
blubber
blowhole
windbreak

bird of prey
talon
falconry
univalve
bivalve
dune
mica
silica
alliteration
Newbery Medal
hyperbole
squall
front
conclusion

Fine Arts
Composition in drawing
Singing
Illustrating correspondence
Thomas Hart Benton, American artist
Drawing birds
Killdeer
Sound effects—squalls

Issues of Human Relationships
Memories
Family activity–singing
Wanting to be liked
Traits and people
Grieving
Making others smile
Always something to miss

George Washington Carver

History

Code of Hammurabi
Babylonia 1700 B.C.
Royal Society of London (for Improving Natural Knowledge), 1660
Chief Black Hawk
Black Hawk War of 1832
Kaw Indians
Homestead Act 1862
Civil War and Introductory Overview
   "The War Between the States"
   "The War of Secession"
   Frederick Douglass
   Ulysses S. Grant
   Robert E. Lee
   Abraham Lincoln
   Confederacy
   Union
   Ft. Sumter
W. E. B. DuBois
Booker T. Washington
Tuskegee Institute (University)
President Theodore Roosevelt
President Howard Taft
President Herbert Hoover
Henry Ford
Joseph Stalin
George Washington Carver Museum and National Monument
Carver's writing
Segregation
Jim Crow Laws
Brown vs. Board of Education
Martin Luther King, Jr.
Rosa Parks
Civil Rights
March on Washington, 1963
Martin L. King, Jr. assassinated
James Earl Ray
Martin L. King Day (federal holiday)
African Methodist Church history
   Richard Allen
   Absalom Jones
Surnames
History of photography
   Traveling photographers
Famous people from MO
   Harry Truman
   Mark Twain
   Walt Disney
   Joseph Pulitzer
   General John Pershing
Postal Service
   ZIP codes
Genealogy, making a portfolio

Geography

Babylonia
Africa
Canada
Caribbean
England
   London
South America
United States
   Alaska
   Homestead Act
   Georgia
      Atlanta
   Iowa
      Hawkeye State
      Buckeye State
   Kansas
      Wheat State
      Topeka, capital
      Wichita
      Fort Scott
      Abilene—Dwight D. Eisenhower
   Missouri
      Jefferson City, capital
      Show-Me State
      Diamond Grove
      Neosho
   Tennessee
      Memphis
   Washington, D.C.

Science

Human body
   Parts of throat
      Larynx
      Vocal cords
Ornithology, the study of birds
Insects
   Identification
Botany
   Photosynthesis
      Chloroplasts
      Chlorophyll
      Glucose
Agriculture
   Crop rotation
   Nitrogen cycle of soil
   Proteins, amino acids
   Legumes
      Uses of
      Nodules
      Bacteria
   Sweet potato
      Uses of
   Peanut
      Uses of
   Gardens
   Horticulture
      Flower
      Vegetable

Skylark, continued

Geography, continued
Michigan
  Dearborn
  Detroit
Mexico
South America
Brazil
Europe
Portugal
Asia
China

Science
Human body
  Heat exhaustion
  Sweat
  Evaporation
  Perspiration
  Heat stroke
  First aid
Genetics
  Traits
  Genes
  Dominant
  Recessive
  George Mendel
Cows—herbivores
  Guernsey, Jersey,
  Holstein, Angus,
  Herefords

Cow stomachs
  Rumen
  Reticulum
  Omasum
  Abomasum
Enzymes, bacteria, proteins
Gestation period in animals
Bird—Loon
Droughts and floods
Weather station
  Rain guage
  Thermometer
  Barometer
  Weather vane
  Measuring wind speed
  Dew point
  Condensation
  Snow
Fire
  French chemist Antoine
    Lavoisier
  Requires oxygen, fuel
    and heat
  Combustion
  Ash content
  Fire precautions
  First aid
Photography
  Camera lens
  Aperture
  Focus
  Latent image
  Silver in film process
  Darkroom

Astronaut
  NASA
  Shuttle
  Airforce, Navy
  Space
Astronomer
  Stars, planets
  Space
  Telescope
  Observatories
  Planetariums
  Percival Lowell
  Edwin Hubble
  Willamina Fleming
Phonograph
  Sound vibration
  Amplification
Wells
  Geologist, Engineers
  Drilling
    Artesian wells
    Oil and gas wells
    Mineral wells
  Seismographs
Water table
  Water source
  Ground water
Dams
  Flood plains
  Drought
  Ground saturation
  Geology
  Water conservation,
    pollution

Water safety
  Lighthouse
  Buoy systems
  Oceanographers, car
    tographers
  Nautical charts
  Electronic navigational
    system
    Loran (U.S.)
    Loran-C (Canada)
Tides and oceans
  Tides and the moon
  Global ocean
    Pacific Ocean
    Atlantic Ocean
    Indian Ocean
    Arctic Ocean

Language Arts
Writer's styles
Learning to interview
Developing symmetry in
  writing
Imagining a sequel
Analogies
Imagery
Author's license

Literature explored:
What You Know First
  by Patricia
  MacLachlan
Three Names by
  Patricia
  MacLachlan

Skylark, continued

Literature explored, continued

Julius Caesar by William Shakespeare

Vocabulary Words

motif
gestation
premature
primary colors
secondary colors
tertiary colors
analogous colors
complementary
rumen
regurgitate
cud
reticulum
omasum
abomasum
land reclamation
heatstroke
heat exhaustion
oxidation
combustion
kindling temperature
analogy
shellac
license
well
ground water
reservoir
water table

global ocean
tides
symmetry
buoy
chart
Loran/Loran C
trait
genetics
dominant
recessive

Fine Arts

Crayons from science
Watercolor painting
Mixing paints
Colors of drought
Creating theatrical fire
Julius Caesar by William Shakespeare
"Hush, Little Baby"—folk lullaby
Ragtime music
Scott Joplin
"Maple Leaf Rag"

Issues of Human Relationships

Avoiding striking back
Optimism and hope
Being a person of commitment
Making rather than buying gifts
Dealing with hard choices
Being part of a family
Working through fears

Career Paths

Astronaut
Astronomer

Helen Keller

History

Robert Fulton
Nautilus
Clermont, 1807—successful
Steamboat
Ship building
Canals and locks
War of 1812
Scarlet fever epidemic
Anne Sullivan
Louis Braille
Braille System
President William Henry Harrison
President James A. Garfield
President Chester A. Arthur
Electric street cars
Perkins Institute
Circus
Ringling Bros. and Barnum & Bailey
Roustabouts
Gunther Gebel-Williams
President Benjamin Harrison

World War II—introductory overview

Adolph Hitler
Pearl Harbor
President Franklin Roosevelt
President Harry Truman
Axis
Allies
Albert Einstein
"Manhattan Project"
Atom bomb
Enola Gay
Hiroshima
Nagasaki
Emperor Hirohito
V-J Day
United Nations
Causes WWI
Treaty of Versailles
Nationalism
Rise of dictatorships

Geography

Africa
North America
United States
Tuscumbia, AL
Pearl Harbor, HI

Helen Keller, continued

Geography, continued
Boston, MA
Plymouth Rock in MA
Baraboo, WI
Europe
Belgium
Denmark
France
Paris
Germany
Great Britian
Italy
Luxembourg
Netherlands
Norway
Poland
Soviet Union
China
Japan
Hiroshima
Nagasaki

Science
Primates
Monkeys (prosmians)
Apes (anthropoids)
Caring for young
Predators
Humans

Human body
Eye, parts of
Orbit
Pupil
Iris
Cornea
Retina
Tear ducts
Eye lashes and lids
Focus
Sight
Blindness
Color blindness
Glaucoma
Cateracts
Glasses and contact lenses
Sensory deprivation
Understanding term "Deaf and Dumb"
Five senses
Taste
Touch
Hearing
Sight
Smell
Sound
Vibration
Doppler effect
Sound interference
Echoes
Atom
Splitting the

Language Arts
Creative writing
Imagining characters' feelings
Persuasive arguments
Etymology—the study of words
Creative writing on spring
Creating characters

Literature explored:
Black Beauty by Anna Sewell
"The Tyger" by William Blake
Sarah, Plain and Tall

Vocabulary Words
etymology
etymon
Braille
Louis Braille
primate
tandem

Fine Arts
The Miracle Worker—movie, 1962
Family Band movie
Juggling
Tea by moonlight
Cooking

Issues of Human Relationships
Living with hope and determination
Fostering anticipation for each new day

Career Path
Speech therapist

Color Wheels- Primary, Secondary, Complementary and Analogous Colors

Directions: Use colored pencils to fill in each of the specific wedges named on the wheels.

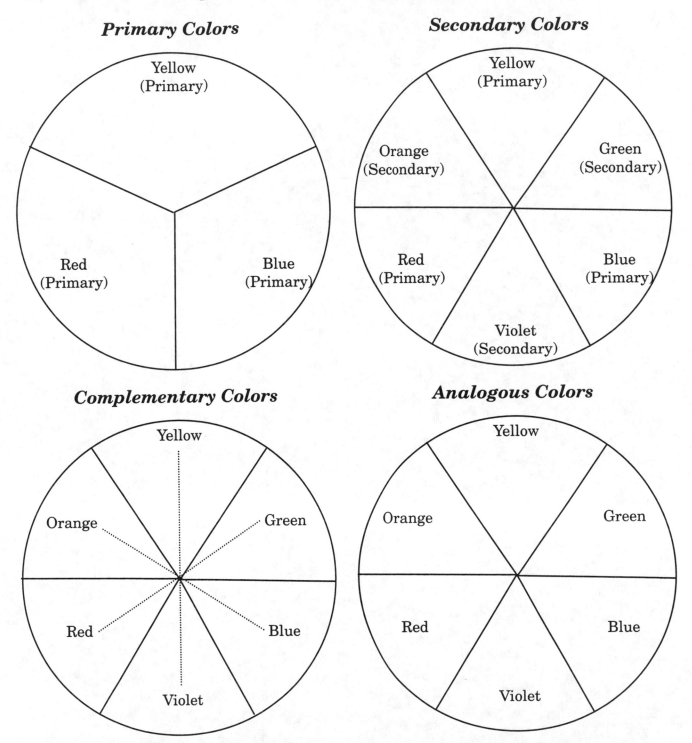

Primary Colors

Yellow
(Primary)

Red
(Primary)

Blue
(Primary)

Secondary Colors

Yellow
(Primary)

Orange
(Secondary)

Green
(Secondary)

Red
(Primary)

Blue
(Primary)

Violet
(Secondary)

Complementary Colors

Yellow

Orange

Green

Red

Blue

Violet

Dotted lines connect each color with its complement, directly opposite on the color wheel.

Analogous Colors

Yellow

Orange

Green

Red

Blue

Violet

Red and Orange are analogous colors, or "neighbors." So are Red and Violet, etc. Analogous colors are any colors found adjacent to one another on the color wheel.

HUSH, LITTLE BABY

Gently

Lullaby

This Award Certifies

that _____

has successfully completed

Beyond Five in a Row, Vol. 2

on this _____ day of _____, 20 ____

Award of Excellence

Teacher _____

Author _Becky Jane Lambert_

Other Products from Five in a Row

Before Five in a Row by Jane Claire Lambert- This treasury of learning ideas was created for children ages 2-4. Enjoy exploring 24 wonderful children's books while building a warm and solid foundation for the learning years just around the corner.   ISBN 1-888659-04-1 $24.95

Five in a Row *Volume 1* by Jane Claire Lambert- Volume 1 contains 19 unit studies built around 19 of the very best children's books ever printed. Each unit takes five days to complete. Created primarily for children ages 4-8 but don't be afraid to include other ages too! ISBN 1-888659-00-9 $19.95

Five in a Row *Volume 2* by Jane Claire Lambert- Volume 2 explores 21 more outstanding children's books. Each unit takes five days to complete. Created for ages 4-8.   ISBN 1-888659-01-7 $24.95

Five in a Row *Volume 3* by Jane Claire Lambert- Volume 3 explores 15 additional outstanding children's books. Each unit takes five days to complete. Created for ages 4-8.   ISBN 1-888659-02-5 $19.95

Five in a Row Christian Character and Bible Study Supplement by Jane Claire Lambert- This wonderful resource teaches hundreds of non-denominational Bible lessons and concepts using the first *three* volumes of *Five in a Row.* Teach your children about obeying parents, kindness, generosity, good stewardship, forgiveness and more. Ages 4-8. ISBN 1-888659-03-3 $17.95

Laminated Full Color Story Disks by Jane Claire Lambert- Each volume of *Five in a Row* contains black and white *story disks.* Use these little half-dollar sized drawings to teach children geography by attaching them to your own large, world map as you explore each new *Five in a Row* story. Just cut out the disks, color and laminate them. *However,* we offer this *optional* set of already colored, laminated disks for those who prefer to save the time needed to prepare their own. These disks are printed in full color and heat laminated—ready to use. One set of these disks covers all *three* volumes of *Five in a Row.* Beautiful and ready to enjoy! $15.00

The Five in a Row Cookbook by Becky Jane Lambert. This companion volume to *Five in a Row* (Volumes 1-3) and *Beyond Five in a Row* (Volumes 1-3) provides complete recipes and menus to complement each story you study. You'll enjoy the opportunity to wrap up each unit with a family meal, a time of celebration, and the opportunity for your students to share their achievements. You'll also appreciate the scrapbook area for photos, notes and homeschool memories.
ISBN 1-888659-11-4 $22.95

Beyond Five in a Row *Volume 1* by Becky Jane Lambert- Here is the answer for all those moms who have asked, "What do I do <u>after</u> *Five in a Row?*" You'll find the same creative, thought-provoking activities and lesson ideas you've come to expect from *Five in a Row* using outstanding chapter books for older children. Volume 1 will keep your students busy for many months with history, geography, science, language arts, fine arts and issues of human relationships. Each unit also includes numerous discussion questions, career path investigations and much more. Volume 1 requires *The Boxcar Children, Homer Price,* and the *Childhood of Famous American Series* biographies of *Thomas A. Edison- Young Inventor* and *Betsy Ross- Designer of Our Flag.* Created for ages 8-12. ISBN 1-888659-13-0 $24.95

Beyond Five in a Row *Volume 2* by Becky Jane Lambert. Requires *Sarah Plain and Tall, The Story of George Washington Carver, Skylark,* and *Helen Keller.* ISBN 1-888659-14-9 $24.95

Beyond Five in a Row *Volume 3* by Becky Jane Lambert. Requires *Neil Armstrong-Young Flyer, The Cricket in Times Square, Marie Curie- and the Discovery of Radium,* and *The Saturdays.* ISBN 1-888659-15-7 $24.95

Beyond Five in a Row Bible Christian Character and Bible Supplement by Becky Jane Lambert- This companion volume to *Beyond Five in a Row* provides a rich selection of the wonderful Bible references and strong character lessons you've come to expect from *Five in a Row.* This valuable supplement teaches traditional Christian values such as honoring parents, forgiveness, generosity, etc. Covers all three volumes of *Beyond Five in a Row* in one handy volume. Effective and easy to use! ISBN 1-888659-16-5 $17.95

Above & Beyond Five in a Row *The First Adventure* by Becky Jane Lambert. This latest offering from Five in a Row Publishing is based on Rachel Field's Newbery award winning book *"Hitty: Her First Hundred Years."* This stand-alone unit study is aimed at students ages 12-14 years of age and includes a wide variety of learning opportunities in the best *Five in a Row* tradition. Each "adventure" will take several months to complete. ISBN 1-888659-17-3 $19.95

Five in a Row Holiday: *Through the Seasons* by Jane Claire Lambert and Becky Jane Lambert *Five in a Row Holiday* is by far our most personal, intimate book, sharing our own family's values, traditions and memories in a way that we hope will inspire you to take whatever seems good to you from our experience and combine it with your family's unique traditions as you create your own family holiday heritage. Filled with individual holiday unit studies, activities, recipes, projects and memories, this book is more than just curriculum. You'll discover a delightful treasury of holiday enjoyment.
ISBN 1-888659-12-2 $24.95

Name_____

Address *_____

City/State/Zip_____ Phone_____

Item	Qty.	Price Ea.	Total
Five in a Row Holiday-through the seasons		$24.95	
<u>Before</u> *Five in a Row* Ages 2-4		$24.95	
Five in a Row Cookbook		$22.95	
Five in a Row-Volume 1 Ages 4-8	pkg	$19.95	
Five in a Row-Volume 2 Ages 4-8	pkg	$24.95	
Five in a Row-Volume 3 Ages 4-8	pkg	$19.95	
Five in a Row Bible Supplement	pkg	$17.95	
Laminated Full Color Story Disks	pkg	$15.00	
Five in a Row Cookbook	pkg	$22.95	
Complete FIAR Pkg. (Save 10%)		**$108.00**	
<u>Beyond</u> *Five in a Row* Vol. 1 Ages 8-12	pkg	$24.95	
<u>Beyond</u> *Five in a Row* Vol. 2 Ages 8-12	pkg	$24.95	
<u>Beyond</u> *Five in a Row* Vol. 3 Ages 8-12	pkg	$24.95	
<u>Beyond</u> *Five in a Row* Bible Supp. V.1-3	pkg	$ 17.95	
Five in a Row Cookbook	pkg	$22.95	
Complete BEYOND Pkg. (Save 10%)		**$104.00**	
NEW <u>Above & Beyond</u> *Five in a Row*		$19.95	
The First Adventure "Hitty" **(ages 12-14)**			
6-Cassette FIAR Conference Tape Set		$32.40	
4-Cassette Steve Lambert Tape Set		$21.60	
Five in a Row Book Tote		$12.95	
Reading Made Easy Phonics		$45.00	
by Valerie Bendt			

<table>
<tr><td></td><td>Merchandise Total</td><td></td></tr>
<tr><td>**Make Check Payable To:**</td><td>Shipping Charges*</td><td>$5.95</td></tr>
<tr><td>*Five in a Row*</td><td>MO Residents add 7.10% Tax</td><td></td></tr>
<tr><td>*P.O. Box 707*
Grandview, MO
64030-0707</td><td>Order Total</td><td></td></tr>
</table>

Thank you for ordering *Five in a Row*